EDUCATION

OF

TO-DAY

T0382565

EDUCATION

OF

TO-DAY

*A Series of Addresses delivered at the
Third Young Public School Masters'
Conference at Harrow School
in January 1935*

Edited by

E. D. LABORDE, Ph.D.

Assistant Master at Harrow School

CAMBRIDGE
AT THE UNIVERSITY PRESS

1935

CAMBRIDGE
UNIVERSITY PRESS

University Printing House, Cambridge CB2 8BS, United Kingdom

Published in the United States of America by Cambridge University Press, New York

Cambridge University Press is part of the University of Cambridge.

It furthers the University's mission by disseminating knowledge in the pursuit of
education, learning and research at the highest international levels of excellence.

www.cambridge.org
Information on this title: www.cambridge.org/9781107678286

© Cambridge University Press 1935

First published 1935
First paperback edition 2014

A catalogue record for this publication is available from the British Library

ISBN 978-1-107-67828-6 Paperback

CONTENTS

FOREWORD

THE present volume contains a series of lectures and addresses delivered in January, 1935, at the third Conference of Young Public School Masters at Harrow. As in 1930, when the Conference was first held, the considered discourses of a strong body of lecturers seemed to deserve, if not to demand, a wider audience than that of the hundred and thirty public school masters who listened to them. The extensive appeal of the volume containing the lectures delivered at the first Conference strengthened the proposal to publish, and it was decided to lay a collection of the addresses before all those interested in education, whether practically or theoretically.

Unfortunately, it has not been possible to include all the addresses actually given, since some of them were informal talks, while others were delivered from short notes which the busy speakers have not found time to amplify for publication. These and the discussions which followed the various lectures have proved useful and stimulating to those who heard them; yet this volume may claim to hold whatever was spoken at the Conference, which the audience felt that it would like to read afterwards at leisure in order to reflect upon and assimilate. Sir Robert Waley Cohen's authoritative address on *Leadership*, which was delivered in 1932 at the second Conference and has remained in manuscript for three years, has been deemed too good to be left in continued neglect and has been included here.

A glance at the list of authors in the Table of Contents will show how varied the outlook of the several lecturers was bound to be. Naturally, the majority of speakers were professional educationists in the schools and universities, but the rest included men of business, science, religion, and social work, who had approached and studied education from the point of view of their own interests. Yet, that variety has not made of the volume a miscellaneous collection of articles, since a large measure of unity has been secured through the direction of the lectures towards the common theme of "Education in an international world"—a phrase whose significance is fully explained by Mr Laurin Zilliacus. In some respects the lectures supplement each other by turning the limelight on to different parts of the same subject. A striking degree of agreement is noticeable on such matters as the need for bringing education into touch with modern life in both subject and method, the special difficulties of the youth of to-day amidst the rapid progress of mechanical invention, or the importance of training the mind to think independently and to eschew catch-phrases and ready-made opinions.

The volume offers a peculiarly representative picture of educational thought in this country at the beginning of 1935. Since the "Harrow Lectures" contained a similar review for 1930, a comparison of the two books carries the interest of enabling the reader to realise and gauge the vast amount of progress made in the science of education during the intervening five years. Perhaps the greatest change is to be found in the loosening of the old academic bonds and a tendency towards realism in education. It is not merely a trend towards a new curriculum that is noticed, but also a new spirit of approach to the studies of the past. Without our noticing it, a revolution has taken place.

The present time is one of tense international stress. A world whose interests are international and which pays lip-service to the principle of co-operation among peoples is paradoxically intensely nationalistic in its outlook and in the economic and political actions of the several States. The holding of a Conference on such a general theme as "Education in an international world" and the attendance of a large and enthusiastic body of masters from a wide range of public schools demonstrates the alertness of the older foundations and their readiness to play their part in solving a world problem. Difficulties exist, and chief among them is the tendency of sectional bodies towards the use of the schools of this country for spreading sectional beliefs. But, as Mr Spencer Leeson says: "the fair-mindedness of the majority of English teachers... will protect us against the grosser assaults of propaganda".

Nothing now remains, except to thank those who enabled the Conference to be held: the lecturers who gave their time freely and ungrudgingly; the Headmaster of Harrow, who again allowed the use of the War Memorial Building and afforded other facilities; the various housemasters who kindly put up a large part of the gathering; the staff of the Hill Tea House; and the many School servants, who gave up a portion of their holidays.

E. D. L.

Harrow-on-the-Hill
September 1935

INTRODUCTION

Lord Eustace Percy

THE present volume contains the addresses delivered at the third Conference of Young Public School Masters in January 1935. No record survives of my own opening address; it deserved none, for every point which I sought to make was better made by subsequent lecturers. As a substitute for it, I have been asked by the Editor to write a word of introduction.

The atmosphere of these Conferences is, I think, well described by Mr Zilliacus on page 96: "A survey of the New Education must include a great deal that is common practice and common outlook throughout English education of to-day and some that has long been so, particularly in the Public Schools.... The boundary line between old and new is not easy to trace in England." It is the absence of this boundary line that sets the tone of all English thinking about education—and, indeed, about social life. Elsewhere, modern ideas and modern needs in education can be discussed in the terms adopted recently by a group of American writers, in terms of an Educational Frontier. It may be the frontier of the American pioneer, a steadily advancing line between farm and prairie, between the desert and the sown. It may be the Front of Nazi propaganda, the battle line of a disciplined community. But, however conceived, it is a boundary on either side of which rival theories can be sharply defined. In England there can be no such clear-cut formulation, for there is no "united front". No doctrine has held long enough to create a school or provoke a counter-school. There has been tradition, but our tradition is a climate rather than a code, and an English climate, where it is good to live, but where outlines are blurred, where the distances of past and future fade into mist, and where man's rawest innovations are quickly softened into the landscape by grass and creeper and tree.

And so, the question to be asked of a book like this is, not "are these views of education conservative or progressive?" but "is this a good climate to work in?" That would be true of the deliberations of any body of English teachers, but Mr Zilliacus is right is using the words "particularly in public schools". Nowhere does the haze of distance veil so many past changes of organisation and even of function, nowhere does the native growth of heath and woodland conceal so many recent experiments of building and quarrying, as in what is sometimes called our public school tradition. And nowhere to-day has the impact of economic change upon the school been stronger than here, nowhere is the need for adaptation to new conditions and prospects of social life more keenly felt. This sense of shock and this effort at response pervade these addresses, and not the less effectively, to a sensitive ear, because they are expressed in so conversational an undertone. In our response, we are not the less alive to formulated principles of education because we speak of "unity of curriculum", as on page 13, under the genial symbolism of the "red herring". Above all, we know that the response required of us is that we should give to our younger generation a fresh sense of purpose; but it is not in our climate, even were it in our conscience, to exalt them into a priesthood or mobilise them into a pretorian guard. We believe, obscurely but with confidence, that their purpose will be set for them by the spirit already in them and by the world as it is around them, and we seek so to bring these two together, the eternal inspiration with the changing environment, that the resulting impulse may deserve to be dignified by the name of Duty.

EDUCATION OF TO-DAY

EDUCATION IN CITIZENSHIP

Spencer Leeson

I AM here to-day on behalf of the Association for Education in Citizenship.

You will find at the bottom of the Hall a quantity of papers in which are set forth the aims and methods of this Association. I will begin by reading out this statement to you. It is as follows:

"To advance the study of and training in Citizenship, by which is meant training in the moral qualities necessary for the citizens of a democracy, the encouragement of clear thinking in everyday affairs and the acquisition of that knowledge of the modern world usually given by means of courses in History, Geography, Economics, Citizenship and Public Affairs."

That is the object which the Association sets before itself; and the methods by which it proceeds are as follows:

(1) "To collect information as to what is being done in regard to training in Citizenship in Schools and in other educational institutions, both in the United Kingdom and elsewhere;

(2) "To compile bibliographies; to maintain a library of suitable books, and to arrange, where necessary, for the production of new ones;

(3) "To compare present methods in training in Citizenship and to work out new ones; to suggest courses; to promote discussion in educational conferences, in the press and elsewhere;

(4) "To make representations with regard to training in Citizenship to bodies having control of education; and lastly

(5) "To co-operate with the Historical Association, the Geographical Association and other kindred bodies as regards common objects."

This is the bare official statement. In what follows I will endeavour to enlarge upon this statement, with particular reference to the three great topics, which if adequately treated would cover the whole matter—namely, the moral qualities necessary to good citizenship; training in clear and correct thinking; and the acquisition of certain kinds of knowledge which every citizen should possess. But it is first necessary to say a word about one fundamental conviction which the Association takes for granted in those who are interested in its work.

The Association is in the widest and broadest sense non-partisan. It tries to unite members of different parties in its service; it does not seek to recommend the dogmas of any political group. But there is one matter in which we are partisans and one dogma to which we hold as to an article of faith. We believe in the English political and educational tradition. What does this mean? It means this. We have never, either in education or in politics, sought to create an artificial mass-type—a body of boys and girls pledged as a matter of discipline to worship this ideal or that. We have never thought or taught in this country that there is one way of thinking about politics or anything else which is right and that all other ways are wrong. We have proceeded on different lines. We believe that the schools should try to train boys and girls in habits of careful, humble enquiry and independent judgment on politics as on other subjects and that it is not our business to mould them to one pattern, to recruit them to one cause, to make them Fascists, Conservatives, Liberals, Socialists, or Communists. We believe in freedom of thought, not indeed as an end in itself, but as a means to a greater end; and we desire our pupils, as members of a free state in which individual personality is respected and individual opinion carefully weighed, to look at public questions as questions which touch not only their interest, but their moral being, as questions to be settled by discussion and consent in a broad spirit of toleration and responsibility and reverence for law. That is the only uniformity we should desire to see.

This is the English tradition of government, and it is reflected in the schools. At no time have they been consciously used as the instruments of a policy. It is quite otherwise in many places elsewhere to-day—Russia, Italy, Germany. There—I am not condemning or even criticising them but simply trying to state what appear to be the facts—the schools are made into instruments of policy. It is not their business to train an independent, balanced, broad-minded judgment, but to turn out enthusiastic recruits for the armies, civil, technical or military, of the totalitarian State. There have been other examples in the past. The system devised by Napoleon for France under the Consulate had the same method and the same end. That is not our end nor is that our method. In education, as in politics, we hold that the object of all activity is to assist the development of the individual soul towards the good, or as I should prefer to say, towards the fullness of God; seeking to make political and economic organisation serve that end.

The individual is an end in himself; the State is not. But the individual cannot attain the full measure of his development except as a member of a community. Therefore, though citizenship—the art of living well as a member of a community—cannot be regarded as the primary end of education, yet it is a secondary end of high importance, and the primary

end cannot be reached without it. How then can we train boys
and girls in citizenship—the art of living well not only in
England, but in Harrow, not only in Harrow, but in the
British Commonwealth of Nations, and indeed in the wider
unity far descried beyond that?

How can this task be undertaken, and how, as practical
teachers, should we tackle it? It falls into three parts. We
must encourage, if we can, the growth in our pupils of certain
moral qualities. We must train them in habits of clear and
balanced and unprejudiced thinking. In the third place there
is certain positive knowledge which every citizen ought to
possess and which the schools therefore must make it their
business to impart.

First, of the moral qualities, the State exists to preserve good
life. The second great commandment given by Christ is not
only a maxim in ethics, it is the supremest wisdom in politics
as well, and to teach this by example and precept must be our
first care. We must make those for whom we are responsible
see that love of their neighbour is something more than a
pulpit platitude; that it will not do to look upon the State
either as a universal provider or as a tiresome intrusion, but a
living family claiming their service. Not "Service to the
Community", as a large and windy abstraction, but service in
this or that concrete form, this or that definite direction. We
must cure them of an unworthy quietism, or desire to live their
own lives in their own way. Their lives are not their own. As
members of a democratic society, public questions are their
concern. It is they who in the last resort direct public policy,
and public policy cannot be soundly based except on the free
consent and co-operation of individual wills, not acting with
an eye to their special interests. Side by side with the duty of
taking broad views, is the readiness to undertake responsibility in different spheres of administration. Much must of
necessity be left to the expert; but it is of the essence of a
democratic state that in it the expert advises, but does not rule.
There is a vast sphere of work open to all here and by one of

the noblest of our traditions practically all of it is unpaid. To this unpaid service, as members of Local Authorities, Hospital and School Management Committees, as Justices of the Peace and in hundreds of other less obvious and more personal ways, our pupils will be called; and it is for us to see that they do not refuse.

The schools have sought to train boys and girls in this sense of responsibility and service. This has been a specifically English contribution to educational practice, and our prefectorial system, our committee system, and the like have been devised with an eye to this end. Indeed so strong have we been for the community and the type, that we have fallen into the opposite peril of overriding the legitimate claims of the individual, and the erratic genius to whom the world owes so much is said to find no home in the English schools. But whatever may be our faults in that matter, we have at least the tradition of service and the means of encouraging it and that for our present purpose is an asset indeed. By itself it is not enough—it needs to be supplemented and reinforced by the possession of certain specific forms of knowledge; and it is apt to assume sometimes a demeanour that is almost patronising—a semi-feudal condescension *de haut en bas*, when what is really needed is a spirit of equal service in the rank and file, and proud to be there—service not 'for' but 'with'.

These are the moral qualities on which true community life, real citizenship is founded. There is no sympathy between them and the qualities on which a dictatorship, whether of the Right or of the Left, can be built. These qualities we need first of all to strengthen in ourselves, and then in those we try to teach, in schools of every sort and kind; and they will bear fruit by God's grace in an eager responsiveness to the calls of public and private obligation and also in a healthy disinterested public opinion operating over the whole field of national and international affairs. Policy will answer for good or ill to the movements of public opinion, as reflected in the press and in Parliament. There was a conspicuous example of this in the forties of the last century, when the conscience of the nation was thoroughly roused over the iniquities of child and female labour in mines and factories, and reform at once followed. There is another shining example of it in our own time—the loud demand from men and women of all parties and classes for housing reform. No amount of machinery will serve unless the spirit is there. When the spirit is there, difficulties collapse like the walls of Jericho. It is for us to help to evoke that spirit.

To moral qualities we must add intellectual qualities; and of these the first for our purpose is the power of clear and balanced thought—not the power of searching out subtle and over-ingenious lines of argument, nor the power of accumulating masses of learning—but the Greek gift of looking things straight in the face and seeing them as they are. In the want of this lies one of the great dangers to intelligent democratic citizenship. We are in peril from propaganda, and the instruments for the diffusion of propaganda are to-day terrible in their efficiency and range. Truth may be distorted and suppressed to serve a cause; events may be torn from their context or actually and deliberately misrepresented because the end is held to justify all means, and citizens need only be told what this or that leader or newspaper editor thinks it good for them to hear. In old days kings used to tune the pulpits; in our time we have seen the press, the cinema, and the wireless tuned so effectively that a whole people can apparently be made to shout with one voice the same words. We have escaped the worst forms of this assault in England, and it is easy for those that try it here to over-reach themselves. But the danger is there. There is a sturdy independence about an Englishman's judgment and a natural distrust of propaganda, as soon as he recognises it as such. But we are not proof against catchwords and slogans, and great masses of men and women may easily be swept off their balance. Our six hundred years of political experience has immunised us to a certain extent, but we cannot claim to be wholly free.

How can education for citizenship insure us against this? It is not an easy question, especially for those schools which lose their pupils at fourteen—and those the pupils who will in the future make up the large majority of the electorate; and unfortunately, it is not always true that the accurate training of the reason in this and that branch of knowledge does anything at all to train the faculty of cool and unprejudiced thought about politics. No doubt, as in every other department, we must depend most of all on the attitude of the teacher, his sense of fair-mindedness, his distrust of vehement partisanship, his strenuous search for truth, and his instinctive shrinking from vulgarity and blatancy wherever displayed. It is suggested from time to time that we should have set classes in formal logic and in psychology, to show how the human mind normally works and to tabulate its fallacies. I feel a doubt about that. We are dealing with immature minds, and immature minds abhor abstractions. It was once said that there should be no set teaching of psychology or philosophy in any schools, but that both should be allowed to 'peep out' from time to time, when the opportunity suited. The skilful teacher will make his opportunities. Something may be done by the analysis of some shoddy piece of thinking in book or newspaper or conversation, so as to illustrate its fallacies. Thouless' *Straight and Crooked Thinking* does this very well. It takes a conversation between three educated men on current problems and shows them falling into all sorts of mistakes, mistakes such as we can hear or make any day in the train, mistakes of prejudice, over-statement, unverified assertion, confusion of metaphor with literal fact, and so forth. Of course the danger of this is that it may lead to priggishness and a horrible, bloodless, superior 'rationalism'. The best guarantee against that is the good judgment and sense of humour of the teacher; and this reminds us again of the terrifying truth that in the last resort it is the character and attitude of the teacher that matters most.

To moral and intellectual qualities we have to add certain

specific forms of knowledge which will make the citizen feel most at home in the world of 1935 and most able to control its currents to good ends. This brings us to the third part of our enquiry. I have no desire to criticise existing schemes of organisation or curriculum, or to plead for a modern course as against a classical course or a science course; the subjects I am going to mention should, it appears to me, form part of the course of every boy and girl for whom anything in the nature of higher education can be provided. What can be done for those who leave the elementary schools at fourteen—the great majority—I have not the experience to discuss; I must leave it to those who know those schools, but I believe they will agree that something on the following lines is roughly what is required, though the conditions under which the elementary schools work—want of time and so forth—would impose many limitations and modifications.

In secondary schools (the term includes public schools) it would, I hope, prove practicable to introduce at some stage or other for all boys and girls instruction in the following subjects:

(i) Modern English and European History—modern in the sense that it merges into current events; the latter to be treated as an organic part of the course, not an occasional frill for a dull period.

(ii) Political and Economic Geography.

(iii) Modern Languages, or to put it in a fairer way, a study of two modern European countries, based on a knowledge of their languages, spoken as well as written; no doubt in most cases the countries would be France and Germany.

(iv) Elementary Constitutional Law, or to put it in a simpler way, How we are Governed; this should have reference to the Dominions and Colonies, as well as to this country. It will explain what Democracy means and what Liberty and Equality before the law mean; and special pains should be taken to describe the machinery which has been devised, by the reform of local government and in other ways, to cope with social problems, and so to bring into view the wide field of service that lies before the citizen in his own town as well as at Westminster.

(v) Economics. Pretty well every political question to-day is at root an economic question. I do not yet feel sure what place should be given in the schools to the teaching of economic theory—as a teaching subject it is in its infancy and we have not yet the experience to guide us; but modern economic history, and what may be called descriptive economics do not present the same difficulty. How many boys know what a trade union is, or what a bank does, or have ever analysed the Budget?

(vi) We should ask teachers of Science to include among their aims the task of explaining what Science has already done and may shortly be expected to do in reducing the demands made on human labour of all kinds. The next age must be prepared for its new leisure before it arrives, else when it does arrive, it will overtake an empty mind. Here is the immense importance of education for leisure. If the prophets of technocracy are right in predicting that at some not far distant time the working day will not exceed four hours, either it is to be a leisure filled with satisfying employment or an *ennui* that will destroy us all. Christ knew the human heart; and when He spoke of the seven devils worse than the first who took possession of the soul that was empty, swept, and garnished, He was speaking of a peril which on a small scale is in the experience of everybody. We must devise in good time some protection against it.

This is what we ask in the matter of positive knowledge; and we shall have to face two objections. First, that there is no time, and secondly, that it is impossible to teach political and economic subjects or even very modern history without a danger of bias in the teacher. These objections deserve consideration.

I do not think the difficulty about time is a serious one, and many schools have been able to overcome it. Several of the subjects can be and are treated in the ordinary course of common-form time-tables and it is simply a matter of the spirit and attitude in which they are approached. Moreover, if we are convinced of the importance, the necessity, of these subjects, we shall agree that time must be found for them, and for all boys and girls, no matter what may be their line of specialisation. Indeed anything that will compel us to modify the rigour of specialisation is to be welcomed; this rigour is one of the chief dangers which education has to face in our time. It benefits neither the subject nor the pupil, and it is based upon a mistaken and even a mercenary view of the purpose of education. Here, as in so many other ways, it is the spirit that counts, not the time-table. If the teachers are imbued with the modern spirit, if they really belong to 1935, it matters not whether they teach Classics or Mathematics or Science or History or Languages; they will find time for the essentials of which I have spoken.

The fear of bias in political and economic teaching reflects great credit on those who feel it. It bears evidence to the fair-mindedness of the majority of English teachers and will always protect us from the grosser assaults of propaganda. What to a Russian or Italian or German teacher would be counted for righteousness—that he was creating in the school a nation of Communists or Fascists or Nazis—would be to many English teachers a sign that they were betraying their trust. This fact is in itself the best answer to the objection. The purpose followed, as I believe, by the majority of the teachers of religion as well as politics and economics is to put before their pupils with fairness as many different views as are held on this subject or that, and not to conceal their own convictions; but to leave the final decision to the judgment of each individual boy or girl. No other method would work with English-minded people; blatant propaganda in schools or universities as a rule defeats its own ends.

I do not think either of these objections are really valid; and the more we consider the signs of our time, the more vehemently, as it seems to me, are we urged to break down the barriers between the schools and the world for which the schools exist. We must all feel the difficulties and the dangers of isolation. Some of us live far away in country districts and it is hard to make our boys realise that there can be such places as distressed areas. Their world flows on quietly, and day follows day with its beginning and middle and end, and seed-time and harvest do not fail. What do Tyneside and the Rhondda Valley mean to these boys and girls? Have they seen shipping lying idle on the northeast coast? Have they seen the unemployed queueing up at the Employment Exchanges for a job? Do they realise that behind each unemployed man in that queue there stands a woman and a family of children, and that of those unemployed men in middle and later life the majority will probably never do another day's work in their lives?

I do not plead that the schools should be made depôts of social service. Boys and girls are there to learn; action will come later. But our efforts should be directed to secure that right action will follow; and a beginning can be made at the schools with the study of social conditions, not as a frill or appendage, but as an organic part of the training of older pupils. A sense of conscious direction—a sense rare among Englishmen—must be brought into it. Visits to the School Mission or to a Toc H training week-end are not just interesting trips; Scouting is not a useful method of learning woodcraft and general handiness, still less a collection of games to keep small boys amused; lessons in Economics and Local Government are not just lessons. All these, and everything else of the same sort, are stages in preparation for a life of service, service not rendered as an act of condescension, but upon an equal footing as members of the same single family. Boys' clubs and Scout troops have to be created and run; the tasks of the great Local Authorities have to be discharged on a lofty plane of unselfish devotion at the expense of our leisure with no thought of personal profit. How can we arouse for the tasks of peace that spirit of passionate consecration which up to now only war has been able to evoke and keep alight for long in large masses of people?

Some will approach the task in the temper of the humanist, for the service of man as man, the last and most splendid term in the series of creation: others, of whom I am one, in the temper of those to whom Christ's command is everything. No man lives to himself and no man dies to himself. We are all members one of another. We are all children of one Father, brothers and sisters in one family where Christ is the eldest brother. And as our minds dwell on this thought, the horizons of our citizenship enlarge beyond the bounds of one country and one commonwealth. Our citizenship is in Heaven.

THE TEACHING OF CURRENT EVENTS

C. H. K. Marten

(This Lecture was originally in the form of an informal talk, and has been revised for publication.)

THE subject I was originally asked to discuss was History, especially its relation in education to the present state of social and international politics. But when I looked at the programme of this conference it seemed to me to be largely concerned with the position of affairs at the present day, and so I asked Mr Coade if I might talk about the teaching of twentieth-century history—and he agreed. Then I began to survey the field, and I found it too vast a one, and I hope I may be allowed to confine myself to one aspect of the teaching of the history of the twentieth century, namely, the teaching of Current Events.

I

Now the first point I would like to make is that all teachers of history in the teaching of past times are, as a matter of fact, constantly referring to the history of the present. That, after all, was the method of the first public school master who taught history—Dr Arnold of Rugby, a hundred years ago. When he was teaching ancient history he was making constant comparisons with modern times; and he was fond, again, of taking for instance the year 15 in two or three successive centuries and making the boys contrast or compare them together so that they might realise the differences or likenesses in the States of Europe in each of the periods in question. Well, there is nothing boys like so much as, if I may make a verb of it, to "red-herring" you. If Dr Arnold had a leaning for comparisons with modern times, you may be quite sure that his boys took good care to encourage him. And if they persuaded him during perhaps an hour supposed to be devoted to one of the duller periods of Roman history to expatiate on some controversial subject of Arnold's day, you may depend upon it that his boys felt that they had had a very successful morning! So it is with history teachers to-day. For instance, if one was studying the relations between France and Germany at some distant epoch, no doubt one would be led on to talk of the age-long conflict of France and Germany over the Rhine frontier and to end with some reference to the Saar. Or, again, if one was dealing with Julius Caesar or Cromwell, parallels with Hitler and Mussolini would no doubt be suggested by various of your pupils. Or if in this coming summer one was making a genealogy of our early kings, it is safe to say that, in this Silver Jubilee year, one would continue it, by request, so as to include King George V!

But, of course, it may be said that such teaching is incidental; and ever since the war there has been a growing movement that "current affairs" should play a greater part in school life. Only last autumn the Historical Association sent out a questionnaire on the subject of "The Teaching of Current Events and its Relation to the Examination System".* The responses are just coming in. On the whole, they show a marked disinclination to have current events included in any external examination, but they are very interesting as showing what is being done in the schools on this subject.

First of all, there are many societies called at different schools by different names, but dealing wholly or in part with current affairs. There are many debating societies, and one I noticed recently discussed a motion "that Hitler should be sent to St Helena"! Then there are societies for the study of current affairs, school historical societies, foreign affairs societies, and twentieth century societies. One school has a Polemical Society, another a Philatelic Society which the headmaster

* See the Summer 1935 number of *History*, the Journal of the Historical Association.

says is very useful for keeping the boys' knowledge up to date.

Then take an example of what doubtless occurs in many other schools. We have at Eton a Political Society which was started during the war. This consists of some fifty members and meets some four to five times in each school term. We happen to be within easy reach of London, and people are very kind about coming down. The society meets in the evening; some speaker is asked down, gives an address for some forty to forty-five minutes and then is asked questions for another fifteen. The boys manage the whole thing—invite the speaker, introduce and thank him, and ask the questions. Sometimes speakers may be a little startled by the questions asked. I remember one of the most upright and honest of our politicians being somewhat startled at the end of his address by being asked by a boy who knew perhaps more about hunting than he did about politics, "Why are all politicians so dishonest?" On another occasion one who was suspected of republican tendencies was cross-examined as to his attitude towards monarchy; he averred, however, his preference for a constitutional monarchy and put it rather neatly by saying that he would far rather have George V as king than Ramsay MacDonald as president.

Then, again, in some schools a junior branch of the League of Nations Union has been started, and sometimes a test has to be passed before new members are admitted. Thus, at one school—it is a girls' school—the candidates for membership must know what the different organs of the League of Nations are, such as Assembly, Council, the I.L.O., etc.; must be able to describe five things that the League has done, and must understand Articles 10, 11, 12, 16, and 17 of the Covenant—the last a rather formidable task as even European statesmen are by no means agreed as to their implications.

Other schools have a model House of Commons or League of Nations Assembly, and one school staged the debate in the

Assembly with regard to Japan and the Manchurian issue. Then a newsboard with current events seems to be a popular institution in many schools. In one school each member of the sixth form is responsible for some country or subject and contributes anything of importance. Another has a newsboard with movable type which is run by the pupils. More than one school makes use of *The Times* illustrations. A rather stupid non-certificate class which cannot use the pen easily is employed in the school to use paste and scissors and to make for the benefit of the rest of the school a summary of the news of the week for the newsboard, each boy being responsible for a section.

Another method of inculcating a knowledge of current affairs is a General Knowledge paper done by the whole school. Thus, at a boys' public school, in a General Knowledge paper on the events of 1933, the boys, amongst other things, were expected to know, besides the winners of the Derby and the Boat Race, who was, in Great Britain, Secretary of State for Foreign Affairs, the Home Secretary, Minister of Agriculture, Leader of the Opposition, Editor of *The Times*; who was the only ruling Queen in Europe, and who was Prime Minister in Spain; what the I.R.A. was, and what was to be associated with the Blue Eagle and so on. A girls' school was more ambitious and put questions in an essay form such as "State the arguments for British payment of the American Debt from the point of view of an American and give the British arguments for non-payment"; and "Explain as fully as you can the failure of the disarmament conference. What, in your opinion, is the right course for England to take?" Needless to say both papers had references to the Dictatorships now fashionable in Europe. In the boys' public school paper the boys had to know, besides the chief officials in Germany, the Dictators or rulers in Portugal, Turkey, Austria, Poland, and the tribe Bamangwato Bechuna; whilst in the girls' school a question on Dictators was put in an indirect form: "'The day of

Democracy is over.' How far do you think this statement true (*a*) at the present time, (*b*) with reference to the future?"

I come on to consider what is done in school hours. In some schools a lecture is given of an hour a week on current events or current problems; others listen to the B.B.C. lectures, such as those on tracing history backwards or on topics of the week. In not a few schools it is the custom to make the pupils prepare a lecture or write an essay and deliver it for the benefit of the rest. For instance, at one school the world is divided into four sections, and the four most experienced members of the class are allotted each a section and deliver each week a short address on any matters of interest; the rest of the class each have a subject and from time to time have to talk about it. Other schools again have regular courses in civics or economics or international affairs; I remember we used to have at Eton a most successful lecturer on civics—and on one occasion the headmaster arrived to find the division spell-bound by the most vivid description of the sewage disposal of one of our great northern cities in its somewhat insanitary past!

Finally, some schools have what is called a Reading School. Boys come either to the school library, or to a master's study if it is well enough stocked, for one period a week, read a book that they want to read, and take it away. And then, the following week, if they have got what they want out of it, or have finished it, they get another. I personally have found there is always a large demand for War or post-War books, and such writers as Winston Churchill or Cole or Harold Nicolson or Snowden or Liddell Hart seldom have their books on my shelves for long.

II

Whether anything more elaborate than what has been described ought to be done, I am inclined to doubt. Perhaps I may refer to some difficulties in the way. First, as we all know, is the lack of time. The curriculum is choked up now, and every subject is fighting for breath. After all, a cleverish boy in a public school has, during his earlier years at all events, to study three languages, Latin, Greek, French, to say nothing of his own; to those languages he must add Science and Mathematics, History, Geography, and Divinity. How is he to fit in any more subjects in his already overcrowded curriculum? And I personally should very much regret if, as some of our more enthusiastic experts have suggested, the study of the history of the past was dropped altogether and the study of current events substituted.

Then a second difficulty is the evanescent character of current events. Take, for example, Reparations. Well, European politics for some twelve years after the War up to July 1932 meant mainly Reparations and nothing else. I remember I had to revise a textbook of mine in the summer of 1932 and to bring it up to date. I decided then that reparations were dead and so confined the subject to a fairly long footnote. If I were revising to-day, I should be inclined to shorten that footnote and merely say that the Allies in 1921 claimed £11,600 millions, were awarded by the Reparations Commission £6,600 millions, and did in all receive £1,010 millions, which was in part paid for by money which Germany borrowed from the United States! Or take the Saar problem —we all hope that before long the problem will be solved and no more will be heard of it. There is a certain danger if you concentrate too much in your teaching on the events of the day that you may be wasting time on questions which will have no interest of any kind for any of your pupils a little later on.

Thirdly, there is the difficulty of knowing what is really happening. I was talking the other day to a distinguished German who assured me that the one object of the Work Camps and so on in Germany was to make the people of Germany "happy and healthy". Is that really their sole object, or are there ulterior ones as well? Who really knows? And in regard to one's ignorance, I have been much struck by two recent books. One was the third volume of the *Life of Chamberlain* which describes his attempt to make an alliance with Germany in 1898. How many people really knew about the project at the time? In the Foreign Office archives there is practically nothing about it and the full story was told for the first time in the autumn of 1934! Then, again, there is the book of Mr Lloyd George who points out how ignorant members of the Cabinet were kept before the War with regard to Foreign Affairs. I dare say you remember the story of the Imperial Conference of 1911, how that Lord Grey delivered an address to the Overseas Prime Ministers on the present state of Europe, and how that Lord Asquith said at the end that the Prime Ministers had heard more about the real state of affairs in Europe than members of the Cabinet knew.* The story may not be true, but if, as appears from Mr Lloyd George's book, Cabinet Ministers were kept in a state of ignorance about Foreign Affairs, and if much of the information essential to them for forming a sound opinion was deliberately withheld, how can teachers in schools be supposed to know what is really happening?

III

Still these difficulties perhaps need not prevent us from trying to do something in the way of current events, and perhaps I may be allowed to refer to some publications I have myself found useful to keep one up to date.

First, for international affairs, the English *Round Table* (publisher, Macmillan & Co., quarterly, 5s. a copy), and the American *Foreign Affairs* (publisher, Council on Foreign Relations, quarterly, $1.25 a copy) I have found very suggestive. The annual report of the Director of the International Labour Office, a report published each year about May

* Mr Lloyd-George in his *Memoirs* says (vol. II, 47) that he can remember no such review of the European situation being given to the Cabinet as was given to the Prime Ministers of the Dominions in 1911.

(publisher, International Labour Office, Geneva), provides a very good summary of the economic and labour conditions throughout the world. Then I should like to say how very useful I have found the publications of the Royal Institute of International Affairs. Even if you are not a member of it you can buy the publications or obtain a reading ticket for a most admirable library, if the authorities have reason to believe you will make good use of it. The Institute publishes annually a review of the previous year; that for the year 1933 is just out—edited by Professor Toynbee it contains some brilliant pieces of writing. Then, bi-monthly, comes the *Journal* of the Institute, consisting of addresses given by various people at its meetings and, no less important, of the discussions upon them; and the *Journal* also has some valuable reviews of books. Then, fortnightly, comes the *Bulletin of International News* which contains one article each number as well as a summary of the news (price 15s. per year). The address of the Institute is Chatham House, 10, St James's Square, London, S.W. 1, and I know it will be glad to help teachers in any way that it can.

Then, secondly, I should like to say something more particularly on social politics. I have found very useful for social history a good many of the Government reports. Take for instance the subject of National Finance. There are three annual summaries published by H.M. Stationery Office. First there is the *Financial Statement* (4d.), the estimate of revenue and expenditure laid before the House of Commons by the Chancellor of the Exchequer when opening the Budget. Then there are the *Finance Accounts* of the United Kingdom (1s. 3d.), published each year in June, which set out in considerable detail the main heads of revenue and expenditure of the financial year ending in the preceding March. Then, thirdly, there is the *Statistical Abstract* for the United Kingdom published each year in January (6s. 6d.), which supplies a wealth of information of various sorts for the previous fifteen years.

Then there are various Government annual reports, such as those on the activities of the Board of Health, or on the Health of School Children, or the Report of the Chief Inspector of Factories. In particular, there are two publications which I personally find of great interest; one is the *Balance of Trade* published each year in February in the *Board of Trade Journal*, and the other is the record of *Public Social Services* published each year in November.

And now as to the teaching of social politics. Here again, as in International Affairs, a master will be constantly referring to the present when teaching the past. If, for instance, he is dealing with the Poor Law of Elizabeth or with the Poor Law of 1834 he will almost certainly go on to refer to the changes in Poor Law assistance made of recent years. I remember when I was at Oxford my tutor, Mr A. L. Smith, afterwards Master of Balliol, gave a most admirable series of lectures to crowded audiences on political and social questions. He took such subjects as Democracy, State Interference, the Poor Law System, Socialism, Free Trade, Local Government, and the like, and treated them historically, and I do not think anybody was able to discover to which political party he himself belonged, if indeed he belonged to any. I tried more than once at Eton to attempt something of the same sort, and I used to think that it was well worth doing, though the difficulty was to find adequate textbooks.

May I give, as examples, two subjects which might be taken? One is the Balance of Trade. Each year towards the end of February the Board of Trade issues a *Balance of Trade* of the previous year. It attempts to regard Great Britain as an individual and to see how she stands. It attempts to estimate the net balance on all transactions of a revenue character between the United Kingdom and other countries, including those transactions originated by Governments as well as those which arise from dealings between individuals. I used to find this return a good method of introducing boys to the subjects of exports and imports, and of invisible exports arising from such things as Shipping, Overseas Investments, and the activities of the City of London.

Then another subject which might be taken is that of our Public Social Services. The International Labour Office published in 1933 (15s.) an *International Survey of Social Services* which contains the details of the social services of twenty-four countries, and contains an admirable summary of our own. Then each November the British Government publishes an account of them (4d.) and of the expenses connected with them. A most interesting course could be worked out with regard to them. The tables show how the expenses of our social services have risen from £36 millions in 1900 to no less than £490 millions in 1932! You may trace in the Social Services how the State to-day watches over its citizens from the cradle to the grave—or rather from before the cradle till after the grave. And in connection with welfare work, no one who is interested in industrial life should omit a visit to the Home Office Industrial Museum at Horseferry Road, Westminster. In the industries and factories under the Home Office there are roughly 150,000 deaths and injuries each year. Yet the accidents could be reduced, so the experts say, by 80 per cent. if the employers and employees really combined in a campaign against them, and in this museum can be seen all the methods employed for the safety, health, and welfare of industrial workers.

But it is time to conclude. Teachers are not omniscient themselves nor can they make their pupils omniscient. And even if one were capable of doing it one has no time to teach boys everything; and after all it would be very dull for them if they left school without having anything else to learn in later life! Perhaps the best one can hope for is that some boys, at any rate, will leave school with a desire to learn more. We can, at school, begin to interest them in current affairs and in social politics. If we succeed in doing that, we shall not altogether have failed in our duty.

THE WORLD'S SOCIETIES

H. J. Fleure

As teachers we must be concerned to give to our pupils, along with knowledge of facts that they will need, some vision of the world into which they have come, some appreciation of the life and personality of the group to which they belong and in which they will do their life work, and some understanding of the social motive powers that keep the groups of men in being and gives them their opportunities as well, it may be, as their difficulties. Underlying this introductory statement is a strong belief that society, the social group, is not the result of the coming together of individuals, in the sense of the 'Contrat Social', but is the fundamental unit for us. Society is older than man, and it is within society that human individuality has acquired its meaning. That individuality has little meaning apart from society. Society depends on its motive power, and that motive power in its turn depends upon some common measure of a vision of the world, of man's place in the universe. This vision changes with the ages, and herefrom arise the chief problems of our time.

The relation of these serious considerations to the recent growth of the teaching of geography is a matter that deserves, even demands, serious attention.

In the Middle Ages the Church, both in its own right and as the heir of imperial Rome, provided guidance and learning for the peoples of Western Europe, and the vision that filled men's minds resulted from the sublimation of folk tradition through the thoughts of churchmen using the Scriptures as their framework. It was a scheme that considered men as offenders on probation, and the little earth as their place of probation had as its centre Jerusalem, directly under the Eternal Throne, which was hidden from view by the blue curtain of the firmament. The *Mappae Mundi* more or less portray this idea of the world, and so do the stained glass windows and sculptures of the cathedrals. The educational schemes of the day were naturally theological, and any information about lands beyond Christendom was vague or, as in the case of Marco Polo, disbelieved.

This mediaeval vision was revolutionised at the Renaissance. Copernicus showed that the blue curtain was the depth of heaven above. The voyages of discovery brought information, made more accurate by the mariner's compass, to supersede the old maps, replacing them by charts setting forth the capes and bays and river mouths that sea captains wanted to locate. As yet, the knowledge of distant peoples remained fanciful and vague, geography became concerned with lists of names important in navigation, and, later on, names and commodities important in the commerce that grew up. Added to this, the revival of geometry led to the improvement of maps and, with the successors of Galileo, to a study of the earth as a planet.

The detailed form of the mediaeval vision was in a sense gone, but the beauty and enthusiasm of the stained glass windows remained not only for the admiration of later generations but also as the index of a spiritual interpretation of the universe, a permanent heritage, however its formal expression may change.

The spread of printing at the same time opened learning to a large laity and brought a revival of the Graeco-Roman vision of the world to stand side by side, and sometimes in rivalry, with that derived from the Scriptures.

Reverting for a moment to the more technically geographical point of view, it is not to be wondered at that, at the Renaissance, geography did not immediately prosper as a mode of human study. Its data concerning peoples of the world were still mixed with fanciful tales, its maps were subservient to navigator's needs, its cartographical theory and surveying were fields for the geometrician's efforts. Education based on the classics became the vogue, while the vernacular, especially in cases in which it was consecrated by the translation and wide circulation of the Scriptures in the common tongue, gathered to itself an ever increasing heritage. Thus the users of a common language grew conscious of themselves as a group, and political movements accelerated this growth of consciousness of kind in the peoples of Western Europe. This led to the development of the historical sense and to the rise of history and literature, eventually largely national history and literature, to a prominent place in education. Of the rise of experimental science and of the study of modern languages much might be said; but this is more particularly an attempt to discuss geography, and so it is permissible to pass on to a sketch of the rise of modern thought in this field. The growth of history as a subject led to the development of attempts to interpret environmental influences. Similarly, the growth of information about peoples and languages led through Montesquieu, whose ideas were apparently based on those of Ibn Khaldun, to Ritter and Rätzel, while the development of physical science led through geology to physical geography and through physics to climatology. In this way several more or less independent disciplines began to focus themselves on the description and interpretation of the phenomena concerning men in their various environments; and von Richtofen in Germany, Vidal de la Blache in France, and Herbertson* in Britain were conspicuous in their efforts to weave these varied strands together. One cannot but add that Vidal de la Blache contributed a fire of poetic enthusiasm that transfused earthly material into a luminous tissue of spiritual concepts.

Meanwhile, another all-pervasive influence has been making old give place to new in most fields of thought, and this is the vision that is traditionally associated with the name of Darwin. Whether or no the factors of evolution that Darwin thought he could perceive turn out to be the real agents of the great

* Names of living persons are not included here.

process, his vision has seized the world of thought. It pictures a continuous stream of influences working from a past beyond even our imagination through the thin veil of the present into the unknown future. For him the great successions of living things have been responding to environmental influences and have been influencing their environments throughout; these ecological relations are for him the very core of the mystery of life.

It was inevitable that his view of ecology of plants and animals should extend itself to man and that human ecology should arise as a subject of thought and should increasingly attempt to understand men, body and soul, grouped and individually.

There was involved here a deep-seated change of attitude and feeling. In mediaeval thought the world of man was, as it were, an enclave separated from the natural world, and in post-Renaissance studies the natural enthusiasm for books helped the theological tradition to keep man apart from, indeed often set over against, nature. Readers of even such a Darwinian as T. H. Huxley will not need to be reminded how this point of view continued to cling to him in spite of all his efforts to seize the new vision which pictures man in nature, men and their works as part of the universal stream through time. The Darwinian sees men responding to diverse environments, prolonging growth in the cool cloudy lands and depending specially on routine in those which suffer from almost perennial steamy heat, but also altering their environments to meet their needs by digging canals to irrigate what might otherwise be a land of wandering herdsmen, or by destroying forests that could harbour only hunters. If sometimes the irrigation system has led to the salting of the land, or forest cutting has exposed land surfaces to undue evaporation and so drawn soluble salts up to form a sterile crust on the surface, that only illustrates the variability of the interaction, the frequent sacrifice of the future to the present, the falsity of the idea of the inevitability of progress.

The study of human ecology has brought out the limited value of work which is merely descriptive of the present; the infinitely thin veil means little by itself. If all men and all their works are products of evolution then it is clear that knowledge of the evolution of the present from the past is necessary to any interpretation. Diverse men in their diverse environments need to be thought of morphologically, chronologically, and distributionally. It is idle to construct anthropology, history, and geography into completely separate subjects. They interweave, and we rarely reach balanced truth without drawing upon all three.

Study of men in their environments has led us to the outstanding fact that man is a social being, that the group or society is the matrix wherein individuality has struggled to develop, and that the continuance of the group is essential if individuality is not to be lost.

The unitary vision of the world that Darwin's thought has spread far and wide has necessarily reacted upon older ideas of an enclave in human affairs wherein the laws of the rest of nature were somehow overruled or suspended; and old ideas which undoubtedly contributed to the social motive power of European peoples have been correspondingly shaken. We are going through a spiritual crisis at least as serious as that of the sixteenth century when the Middle Ages were dissolved away by the Renaissance.

In the crisis the common measure between men, even within the same linguistic or national group, is often being lessened almost to vanishing point, and it is on that common measure that the essential social motive power depends. We need not therefore be surprised, however we may sorrow, that compulsions by powers-that-be are made rigid even to the point of besmirching the fine flower of individuality. In their perplexity groups are sacrificing that freedom of criticism by individual members which has so often been shown to be the one tonic that keeps the body politic healthy. An enforced uniformity is, in spite of experience, made the sign of the group's existence, and aims and efforts are put forth to express the group's distinguishing characteristics, with the danger of cutting it off from the general stream of civilisation. These may be looked upon as crude attempts to find a new social motive power now the older ones are shaken. To understand the situation it is therefore obviously necessary that we should study societies of men in their diverse environments, in other words that we should seek to understand human ecology more thoroughly and more comprehensively. We must try to see what is the common measure of the mass of the members of each group and what has thence grown to be the social motive power of each group. That, in our own adult thought, is the study into which geography, in association with anthropology and history, is now developing,

It behoves us first and foremost to go beyond what has too often been deemed a sufficient geographical treatment, namely, a survey of physical and vegetational features, a demographic description, and some salient facts of commerce. There is pervading all the study of a group the activity of minds stored with traditions that impel men to act in diverse ways, to dream dreams of a future of greater wealth or power or ease or happiness or freedom from external compulsions. The diversities of those dreams do not merely reflect the diversities of environment or of the *Zeitgeist*, they are products of action and reaction between the self-conscious group and its environment sometimes working through long periods of time.

Let us think of a few examples. In France the sunny summers give a better assurance of wheat harvests than can be gained in most parts of Britain, and the farmer's life may be enriched by apple and pear, peach and apricot, and even the vine. Small wonder then that the French peasant worships "la sainte terre de France" and has struggled, even through revolutions, to secure his hold on the soil. Again, he has not been much drawn away, as was his British neighbour, by the lure of great coalfields and their industries. He has remained a peasant, and even the '*bourgeois*' of the small town is often a peasant at heart, sometimes with the traditional peasant's carelessness about sanitation and scientific nursing. It is a marked feature that, with a birth-rate much higher than that of Britain, the moderate population of France remains almost steady; whereas the already too large* population of our country will apparently still increase for a few years unless the birth-rate falls still more.

The peasant accustomed to exchange goods and services uses relatively little money and hardly needs a bank. Small sums mean much to him, and there is now therefore a serious disjuncture between him and the national government caught in the international stream of expanding figures, bound to talk of billions of francs where of old millions seemed already so large. The peasant has as his ideal maintenance rather than adventurous expansionism, and France is correspondingly the country of small dispersed industries without the urge towards indefinite enlargement that has drawn Britain into a rather unbalanced state of population and into over-dependence on export trade. It is of course true that there are great industrialist organisations in France, but it is also true that they are not the core of the country's activity. The peasant, the market town gathering around its church, the individual shops and small factories, all these are French characteristics, however they may now be endangered by the spread of the motor car and the disjuncture mentioned above. Social continuity underlying revolutions at the surface, a stubborn defence of the sacred soil, a certain amount of disregard for matters outside France, a tendency to occupy leisure in arts and thought instead of in the planning of financial adventure, these are widespread characteristics that not seldom make it difficult for the French and ourselves to understand one another's schemes in public, and especially in international, affairs. Add to this the fact that England's mediaeval aggressions gradually brought to birth a national

* Too large under our present economic system.

group-consciousness in France that has been fed by, and has in its turn fed, the love and worship of the soil, until patriotism has become intense and has expressed itself in a centralised scheme of government that leaves little room for the local initiative we in England perhaps overprize; and that makes the responsibility of the administration to the common law far less marked than in England, where this same responsibility is often looked upon as the main bulwark of liberty. Students of France will realise how these ideas work out in the life, and even on the maps of the country and of its departments, towns and villages, with Paris as the nerve centre of the whole and yet not really typical of the peasant nation. It has been brought back time after time from its revolutions to the old long-trodden path, even if names and organisations have been altered in the crises.

It is often said of Spain that the supply of energy is around the periphery while the centre is half empty, with results that make for unity, make even the maintenance of a self-conscious national group, difficult. Add to this the fact that centuries of religious wars held back both the rise of a middle class and the growth of that freedom of conscience which is so important for the health of society, and we have some notion of the country's difficulties. Again, Madrid, instead of being a concentrated expression of a long tradition, like Paris or our own incomparable London, is a late creation that found its work very difficult, especially before the railway came to its aid. But Spain seems to have awakened, and she finds herself now untrammelled by huge industry; so perhaps by and by she may be able to develop along new lines, avoiding the mistakes we have made, even if her heritage hinders her from following some of our more successful leads.

Germany has its northern, or Prussian, plain separated from the larger southern basins of the Main, Rhine, and Danube, by the *Mittelschwelle*, with its valleys that run among the hills and make up the old-time tangle of small principalities and powers, lay and ecclesiastical, of middle Germany, so long a difficulty in the way of the growth of national consciousness and unity. In what had been imperial Roman territory west of the Rhine and south of the Danube Catholicism remained strong, ecclesiastical princes maintaining the ancient heritage. On the Prussian plain the Roman link was less intimate and Protestantism established itself. In the hills and valleys of mid-Germany, some districts in which cities had been founded by early mediaeval churchmen, such as Münster, Paderborn, Söst, Fulda, Würzburg and Bamberg, have remained Catholic, while in other parts Protestantism has been substituted. Thus, the divergences based upon physiography were accentuated by religious evolution, and Germany long retained a mulplicity of minor rulers who encouraged the arts, and especially music, but delayed national unity until the railway made it imperative and Bismarck appeared. The coincidence of the rise of nationalism with the growth of industry and the spread of the railway network gave that movement a special colouring. It included, one might say, the whole of life in its sweep and gave its neighbours the fear of aggression from the overflowing enthusiasm and tireless activity of its rapidly increasing population. We all know the tragic result and the psychological crisis that followed it. If we think out these points one stage further, we shall have some understanding of the present situation which is so full of difficulty both for the overgrown population* and for neighbouring peoples who cannot but fear aggression once more.

This brief survey of some of our European neighbours shows us how vital it is for us to study the life of human groups in the hope that we may thereby help to construct a scheme in which aggression and the fear of aggression, whether military or economic, shall not merely be kept in check, but shall even be eliminated from the desires of the leaders and especially of the leading nations whose notions of prestige are the chief danger to the peace of the world. A Balkan politician recently remarked with great truth and some wit that the rivalries of the great powers have long been the greatest danger to peace in the Balkans.

* Under present economic schemes.

The same need for exorcising the spirit of aggression from the political, economic, and intellectual worlds forces itself on our attention when we consider the ancient civilisations outside Europe. The peaceable Chinese peasantry feel their ancient family tradition undermined by the great White Peril with its factory goods and military power, and now Japan—standing up to the same Peril with astounding success—is imitating Europe in aggression upon China. The Chinese households with their self-contained economy built up a society that has gone on already for thousands of years and, left to itself, might have gone on for thousands more. It was non-aggressive, so it needed only a minimum of government. Its leaders found satisfaction more in beauty than in power, so armies were of small account. Will it now be forced to develop patriotism of our type? Its neighbour Japan with a civilisation deeply indebted to that of China has yet evolved divergently. A long struggle on a narrow front marked the advance of Japanese power through the long main island (Hondo) and gave rise to a hierarchical military society looking up to the sacred person of the Mikado as the embodiment of the intensely national spirit. The advent of the famous *Meiji* in the mid-nineteenth century with a vision of the utilisation of that religious nationalism is one of the romances of mankind as well as the source of some problems that are insoluble save in so far as temporising may postpone crises until the furious growth of population abates.

In intertropical Africa native societies, almost inevitably dependent on a routine of cultivation, are feeling the impact of international trade. Clothing, knives, and matches are spreading everywhere as index marks of the new contacts. Subsistence cultivation is deeply affected by schemes for cash crops. Communal and tribal land tenure, hitherto the basis of society, is undergoing alteration, wage labour is spreading, railway and motor car and aeroplane are developing a new mobility of goods, services, and men. We Europeans who are bringing all these novelties into old schemes of life unprepared for such a revolution have great responsibilities. It is our duty to study the various relations of native societies to their environment and to see that our innovations do not merely wreck the social motive power of the African who is inevitably waking up to demand his rights as a human being.

In America and elsewhere a transplantation of European social tradition has taken place and has set aside the older native life. The rapid provision of equipment in cities, railways, and other appliances of modern life has left some of the new communities deeply in debt, and to pay interest they have been forced to ensure a large surplus of exports, so as a result there has been a development of expensive local industries. Moreover, this rapid provision of equipment has clearly weakened the old pioneer spirit, and has thus hindered settling the land on a subsistence basis, in fact a contrary movement to the port-cities has become a marked feature in some British Dominions. Here again are matters for study, matters that involve considerations of trade and exchange and especially of world finance and schemes of capital and interest. We have, in fact, problems all over the world arising from the quest for profit and for power. They are difficult to solve because that quest has intertwined itself with the incentives to production and exchange. And yet we know that, if those incentives could be disentangled from the aggressive tendencies that are so widespread, there is abundance available in the world for an even larger population than the present one. That is one difficulty; another is the fact that no one scheme will meet our crisis. The groups of mankind have become so diverse that they need different policies. We must study sympathetically the social life of the people of every part of the world, see what is the social common measure that gives rise to the motive power of each, and work so that we hinder nothing by aggressions, whether political or military, economic or financial, that create reactions of fear and hate. We must remember that peace is possible only to men of goodwill.

THE TEACHING OF THE CLASSICS

Cyril Bailey

THE teaching of the classics suffers from an inherited tradition. Those who teach the newer subjects of education—English, modern languages, natural science, geography—have had the advantage of thinking out their purpose and methods from the beginning, but we have received a tradition of the classics as the one and only form of education, which under modern conditions we have had gradually to adapt and modify, and so to work our way sporadically and bit by bit to a new emancipation. It is therefore well that from time to time we should take stock of our position and consider our purpose and methods afresh.

We must begin by distinguishing carefully—far more carefully than is sometimes done—between the specialist, for whom the learning of the classics is the main basis of education, and the non-specialist, for whom it is incidental. The aim of teaching is in part, but not wholly, the same in both cases, but the methods should be quite different. In teaching the specialist we are trying to give him not only those qualities which are peculiar to a training in Greek and Latin literature, but those also which are the common aim of all education, accuracy, power of thought, the capacity to realise a problem and work towards a sane and sound solution. These latter qualities the non-specialist presumably acquires elsewhere and to him we want to give something of the feeling and character of classical poetry and prose, something of the literary precision and wide humanity which they bring with them; it should be our hope that these may fill a portion of his mind and rouse a love which may encourage him to maintain and pursue his classical studies.

Let us first consider the specialist. How can we best pursue those common aims of education, contributing at the same time towards the more special gifts of classical knowledge. And first, accuracy, which is not only of immense value for the formation of the mind, but also for true literary appreciation: we cannot really grasp poetry, unless we can follow constructions and have the 'feel' of words which comes from knowing their history. The start must be with grammar. The revived interest in the literary aspect of the classics has of late years produced an attack on 'gerund-grinding'. Pupil and teacher alike find it tedious and are anxious to get on. But we must stop and make certain; if the foundations are weak, the edifice will totter. A boy may have a profound feeling for literature, but he will never really be a scholar unless he has a tight grip on the language. Can this drudgery be in any way humanised? In its more advanced stages I submit that it can in at least two ways. Firstly, grammar can be taught not so much as a series of rules, but as an analysis of meaning. There is really only one rule of grammar, that 'you say what you mean'; this is what writers are always trying to do, and the learning of grammar is—or should be—the continuous effort at discovering their meaning and realising how, in a particular medium, they were bound to express it. And secondly, individual authors have their individual grammar; Homer and classical Greek, Plautus and Virgil differ from each other in their methods of speech, and the tracing of new developments and the abandonment of old habits is a fascinating form of study which will make its appeal to most students.

For the teaching of accuracy I should maintain that the practice of composition is vital. You can never get inside a language without trying to write in it; to drop composition is a loss in real understanding. And I would specially plead for the retention of verse composition; it is an incalculable aid to the appreciation of poetry and to many boys a far more attractive form of composition than prose. It is constructive and creative, and its formal and structural elements are much more easily realised. The structure of a hexameter is a far simpler matter than that of a Ciceronian sentence with its rhythmical *clausula*.

Learning by heart has much to do with accuracy and it is a pity that it has of late largely dropped out or diminished. It is far easier to learn by heart in early life and what you learn then lives with you. Here I should like, perhaps irrelevantly, to air a private grievance of my own, that boys come up to the university almost completely ignorant of mythology, not only of obscurer persons like Callisto, Phrixus, and Leucothoe, but even of Jason, Theseus, and Sisyphus. This often places them at a great disadvantage in dealing with an 'unseen' and deprives them of one line of insight into the Greek imagination.

The power of thought. That, I believe, at the schoolboy stage, is often best learned through composition and translation. The comprehension of the structure of a piece of Cicero or of Burke, the capacity to follow out the argument and reproduce it in another medium, the sense of words as a vehicle of thought, all these are probably the best test of reasoning powers at this stage. An experienced examiner once said to me that he would always, in a scholarship examination, choose the candidate who was likely to do well in philosophy in 'Greats' on his Latin prose. But apart from this, a schoolboy's reading of Plato, Thucydides, Cicero, or Lucretius will give him abundant scope for training his reasoning powers; if he is to read intelligently he must follow the argument and understand its drift. Such authors should never be taught as so much 'construe', but always with careful attention to the argument and with strict criticism of its validity.

Thirdly, the capacity to deal with a problem may be acquired in discussing any passage in poetry or prose where the meaning is uncertain, but perhaps it is obtained best through textual criticism. This is often dealt with far too vaguely in sixth form teaching. The non-committal statement of a *varia lectio* is insufficient and wholly unsatisfying. Why should not boys be given a general idea of the way in which classical texts have been transmitted to us? Why should they not tackle in a simple form the relations of the MSS. of a particular author whom they are reading? The Medicean Virgil, the Laurentian Sophocles, Lucretius' O and Q will all provide an easy basis of teaching, and of many of the great MSS. there are now facsimiles available, some of which at least every school library ought to possess. To many boys the weighing of MS. evidence and the sifting of conjectures ought to be a fine exercise of the mind, and to some it should prove a new and fascinating interest.

So far I have been merely regarding the classics, like any other subject, as a means of education and training of the mind, aiming at results which might be attained equally well or possibly sometimes better in other subjects. But we must consider also its own special gifts, which in their broader aspects are much more fully realised nowadays than they were in the more technical era of teaching forty years ago.

First of all they provide a marvellous introduction to the study of humanity and the history of human beings, their actions, thoughts, feelings, religion, and morals. And as compared, for instance, with the study of modern history, there is the great advantage that in the classics these things are 'writ small' in the life of the Greek state and even to some extent in the Roman empire as compared with the vast dimensions of the modern world. Let the study of the classics then be brought into relation with modern things, not in any too direct insistence that 'history repeats itself', but with an eye on the parallelism of problems and solutions. Hitler is not an Augustus reborn, but he does afford some interesting points of comparison and also of contrast. In reading a literary work with boys, set it in the light of history; and, conversely, in teaching them ancient history, illustrate it from literature. The great advance in recent years of our knowledge of ancient archaeology, architecture, sculpture, painting, and the remains of ancient sites affords a special opportunity of illustrating ancient literature and making the social and religious life of antiquity more vivid. It is attractive to boys, because the concrete is always easier to grasp than the abstract, but it should be regarded as the handmaid of literature and not allowed to bulk too large. Remember that pregnant sentence in J. S. Phillimore's inaugural lecture at Glasgow: "I had rather that a pupil of mine should be able to construe one book of Homer correctly than date all the pots and pans in the Peloponnese."

Then, the classics should foster the wider literary sense, a feeling for the structure of a drama or a speech. Plot, character, motives should be understood and not lost sight of in the details of work. Contrast and comparison help much in this and give body and reality to criticism. Do not let the books studied last year drop out of your pupils' memory; let them apply them to what they are reading this year.

And, lastly, there is the narrower literary sense, the sensitiveness to words and to expression, the 'feel' of great poetry which grips a man's mind and stays with him for life. We should never hesitate to encourage this in our pupils. It comes to them often with adolescence as a new revelation. 'Style' was till then something mysterious, a kind of polish which you added to a prose, and now they see it as the very essence of good writing. In many ways they can be helped in this, most perhaps by welcoming their own efforts to exhibit it in prose or translation, though they will sometimes need pruning too.

If we are to awaken all this—or even part of it—in our pupils there are two essential requisites in the teacher. Firstly, his own love of classical literature. If we have not ourselves the fire and the enthusiasm to see the depths of the masterpieces of Greek and Latin, their wisdom, their clarity, their fun, we cannot communicate to our pupils what is most worth having. There is a well-known 'grammar gobbet' in Plautus illustrating a strange use of the preposition *de* : *studio de meo studia erunt vestra*; it has the right relation of teacher to pupils in a nutshell. And if this love is to be kept fresh in us, it must be constantly renewed. Therefore, secondly, we must always be learning ourselves; the vitality of teaching depends on constant progress in knowledge. It need not be that we are learning just the subject taught, but the consciousness that we are still learning ourselves makes it possible to convey the spirit of inquiry to others. I feel bound to say with much hesitation that I do sometimes find schoolmasters wanting here. They are too apt to be content to rest on their undergraduate knowledge of the classics and hand that on without progressing further. The learned classical schoolmasters of the older generation, Arnold, Wickham, Page, are largely a thing of the past. I know that many will plead lack of time; the term is packed full, the holidays are short and must be spent in real recreation. I will not combat this, but only say that where there is a real love of knowledge, "love will find out the way". Niebuhr, speaking as the researcher who also taught, once said "My pupils are my wings, without which I cannot fly"; to those of us who are primarily teachers he might have said "You cannot teach your wings to fly, unless you nourish the body." Teaching and learning are both at their best when they go hand in hand. The universities may be making a mistake in the modern practice of electing research Fellows who do not teach. The schools will make a worse mistake, if they rely on teachers who do not learn.

When I pass to the 'non-specialist', I speak with much greater hesitation, partly because my own experience is very limited, partly because I doubt if the ultimate problem has ever really been faced. We ought to think out what our purpose is and then to derive our methods accordingly. The 'non-specialist' used to be treated as a specialist beginner and taken as far on the specialist round as he could go, much as a classical boy who wished to learn something of science would be taught the elements of specialist chemistry and learn such atomic weights as he could hold. We have got beyond that stage, but ideas are still rather hazy. Our real aim should surely be to give the boy who is not making classics his main study something of the sense of language and, what is more important, something of the sense of literature. Here again a foundation of grammar is absolutely necessary, but it need not be built so high. Perhaps the translation of sentences into Latin and Greek is necessary in the earlier stages to ensure a grasp of grammar and its main constructions, but in later stages composition might well be jettisoned; it is essential to get on to reading, and to comparatively fluent reading. To this end may I hazard a few concrete suggestions?

Firstly, I would sanction the use of translations under some restrictions, and, much as I personally dislike them, I believe that editions with vocabularies are useful. The boys should be able to get at the meaning of what they are reading as soon as possible, and for them the insistence on looking words out in the dictionary, invaluable for the specialist, may be relaxed.

Secondly, in order to cover ground, I believe that the practice of interspersing construe of Latin and Greek with pieces read in English, as in the 'Clarendon' series, is useful. It enables the boys to get on with the story or the argument and keeps interest and attention alive. I should not hesitate to read a complete play with them in a Gilbert Murray translation, so as to give them the structure and feeling of a Greek tragedy before they try to tackle one for themselves.

Thirdly, it is most important that they should get on as soon as possible to the great authors. For this reason I venture to suggest that it might often be well to make Greek the 'non-specialist' language and not Latin, because its writers will make a more immediate appeal, and even in the elementary stages there is an attraction about a language with its own alphabet.

And in Greek why not begin with Homer? Homeric forms no doubt seem odd to those brought up on Attic, but would they, if you started on them? After all, they lay a much better historical foundation for the study of accidence and syntax. And there can be no doubt that the *Iliad* and *Odyssey* will at once win a boy's heart. I remember a schoolgirl, who was beginning Homer, saying to me, "Homer is so funny; he never lets you make a mistake about what he means. He says 'he blinded him in the eye'; of course he did, but how nice of him to say so." And in prose why not start with Herodotus, so full of good stories and simple thoughts. It is often those 'parasangs' of Xenophon and the first struggle through a Euripides play which is so damping to enthusiasm.

The Latin authors were unfortunately not nearly so careful of the interests of the English schoolboy, and it is hard to know where to start. But again Caesar is apt to be repellent, and among poets Virgil is too difficult in his thought for beginners; he is essentially an adult poet. Parts of the *Metamorphoses* perhaps and stories taken from the *Fasti,* or better still the simpler poems of Catullus, might be tried, and in prose Livy, though he is harder, is much more attractive than Caesar; the stories of some of the great heroes, Coriolanus, Cincinnatus, Scipio, might be extracted and large parts of the Hannibal books are splendid and might be a little simplified.

Perhaps you will say to me at this point: "This is all very well, but the examination system opposes fatal barriers to such a free course; the demands of the School Certificate must rule the curriculum." I would answer: "Think out your true purpose and produce a reasoned scheme, and then examining boards will listen to you." They are not nearly so sure of their own ground as you might imagine and not averse to trying reasonable experiments.

I suppose there are moments when each one of us is inclined to have his doubts as to the value of the teaching of the classics. Our critics are always ready to express their doubts, and indeed they are no new thing. In the seventeenth century Bishop Burnet once said that it was "a great error to waste young gentlemen's time so long in learning Latin by so tedious a grammar". The true answer to such doubts was given recently by a former pupil of mine who had gone into business and was in the habit of bringing a Homer or a Virgil in his pocket to the office. His colleagues twitted him; there might be some sense in learning modern languages, but what was the use of this Greek and Latin? "No use, thank God", he replied. Perhaps he went too far but all the same he was right. The value of a classical education does not lie in its immediate usefulness, and any attempt to defend it on that ground is futile. It has a much higher aim than any vocational purpose, the training of the mind and character to meet life and its problems and the filling of the mind, as Plato has it, "with breezes blowing from pleasant places". And on this ground we may claim, firstly, that as training it is at least as good as other systems and has in it all the necessary elements which make for accuracy and power of reasoning, and that over and above that it has a wide human interest and those gifts which only a love of good literature can bring. In the epitaph on a great teacher of philosophy who was also a great scholar it is said: "He loved great things and thought little of himself, and, seeking no disciples, he taught to many the greatness of the world and of man's mind." We classical teachers will have done our task, if some fraction of these words can one day be said of us.

THE WIDER POSSIBILITIES OF PHYSICAL CULTURE

L. P. Jacks

M y interest in physical culture originates in a belief I have long held, that the right method of educating human beings is not the method now practised, either in the Public Schools or in the others—allowing for exceptions to be found here and there. Doubtless the prevailing method has praiseworthy points, but those who praise it judge by standards which the method itself has created, and are themselves products of the method they are praising. Judged by the very different standard of its relation to the real needs of humanity and the boundless possibilities of human nature, it seems to me to reveal at many points a prodigious waste of energy and an astonishing misdirection of effort. On the whole I cannot persuade myself that the right method of educating human beings is provided by the present mix-up of academics and athletics, of lessons and games, of religious instruction and military drill.

In addressing an audience of public school masters I must not forget the great differences that exist between education as it goes on in the schools you serve and the education offered in the State-aided schools to the children of the masses. At the same time both types of school obviously belong to the same system and have many points in common. Both of them are dominated by standards of education which originate in the universities. In the public schools you are working on lines which lead on to university distinctions or at least to a university course. The State-aided schools do the same, though perhaps less conspicuously. In these schools everything leads up to a school certificate, or a matriculation test, the terms of which are fixed by the universities; it comes at the end of the secondary stage, the primary stage leading up to the secondary, so that the whole process falls within one framework, and converges towards one point. It is hardly an exaggeration to say that the whole of our juvenile population, rich and poor, is being educated as though it were destined to finish off in a university. This means of course that for the great majority the process is an unfinished one; it stops far short of its goal; the full harvest of Latin and algebra, history, literature, and science is never reaped. What proportion of public school boys go to universities I do not happen to know: of course it is much larger than in the others. But in a secondary school I recently investigated I was told that out of the 600 pupils not more than three or four pass on annually to the universities.

On the physical side there is much difference between the two types of school, but with an underlying resemblance. In the public schools physical culture goes on mostly in the form of games and athletics; in the State-aided schools it runs rather to periods of drill not always under competent instructors. In neither type has the physical culture anything to do with the final tests at the gateway of the university—except so far as it helps to keep the candidates in good health, though I am told that in Oxford discreet questions are often asked about the athletic qualifications of candidates for scholarships. It falls outside the current of education proper, a sort of beneficial extra, commonly thought of as exercise rather than education. The principles that govern it—if any are recognised—are unrelated to the principles governing the mental or academical sides. The two things are uncoordinated: the mental on a higher level and the physical on a lower; and the lower is often left to instructors whose qualifications are somewhat elementary. For example, in one large school I am acquainted with, the physical instructor and the night watchman is the same person—the arrangement being regarded as fully adequate by the governors of the school, and I suppose by the parents who foot the heavy bills for their children's education. In a school I attended many years ago our games master was a university athlete who had played for his college, but mostly failed in his examinations. He was fond of taking us for cross-country runs which were so exhausting that I remember we used to fall asleep at evening prep., with the result that the Latin prose next morning was unspeakably bad. This was called "keeping a sound mind in a sound body" and was justified on the ground that it took the devil out of us, which no doubt it did, though it quenched the divine spark at the same time.

I mention these things as revealing the estimation in which physical culture is commonly held both by professional educators and by the public at large. It is regarded as necessary but inferior, following the ancient tradition that the mind is a celestial thing and the body terrestrial. The two in consequence tend to fall apart—even to the extent at times of being in opposition—the conflict between the academic and the athletic interests of which we hear so much in public schools and universities. So deeply rooted is this idea of the relative importance of the two sides that a person who pleads, as I do, for their equality and the need of integrating them, is apt to fall under the suspicion of wanting to lower the aims of education. Quite recently, after some remarks of mine had been reported in the newspapers, an Oxford don wrote to *The Times* that he hadn't the remotest idea of what I meant, but that evidently I was no friend of sound learning. I can only trust that my explanation of what I mean will not cause you to regard me in the same light. I contend that for educational purposes the mind and body of the pupil should be treated as an inseparable unity and that no education given to the one can be fully effective unless it supports the education given to the other. I would bring the body along with the mind into the main current of education and would never entrust it to instructors whose status and qualifications were inferior to those of the academic staff. My physical instructor would be a humanist and a psychologist, and the one essential truth dominating all the others which psychology has to teach him would be this: that the organ of human intelligence is not, as many think, the brain alone but the whole body from the crown of the head to the sole of the foot.

Education on these lines would not be addressed exclusively to a thing called 'the mind', that is to an abstraction, but to the whole man, the whole boy, who is a reality. I maintain that integrated education of this kind should be made accessible to every member of the community on the same terms as reading and writing now are. To prove that these things are not fantasies I would point to countries like Sweden and Italy, where physical culture has become a national enterprise, and national institutions are founded to promote it—the great Central Institute in Stockholm, for example, where the art of correlating the two sides is being studied in all its aspects, and a scientific physical culture worked out on that basis. I would point also to accumulating evidence that, in schools where these methods are adopted, not only are the lessons more quickly learnt, and the Latin prose better done, but the games more skilfully played and the athletics on a higher level.

The chief difficulty, in this country at least, is the dearth of competent instructors. Instructors of the school janitor type can be found in plenty; but the highly educated men who are alone competent for the job are very rare, though the dearth is less, I am told, among women, and I am glad to say that the new College of Physical Training in Leeds is doing something significant to remedy the deficiency among the men. I believe the day is coming, though I may not live to see it, when a new profession will form itself on these lines, a profession to which the very best type of our young men and women will find themselves attracted. It is in that direction more than in any other that I look for the reform of our educational system which I have long been convinced needs rethinking out and reconstructing from top to bottom. At present the difficulty of reforming it arises in the main from its self-perpetuating character, from the fact, I mean, that those who carry it on are themselves its products, often with no idea that human beings can be educated in any other way than that in which they have been educated themselves. I hope I am saying nothing unpleasant. But when the other day I was told, in that secondary school I spoke of, that nearly all their prize scholars intended to become teachers under the same system, it was suddenly revealed to me how self-perpetuating the whole thing is. Nevertheless I am hopeful that reform will gradually creep in from the direction I have indicated. Indeed I can see it creeping in even now.

A distinguished educator from the continent was recently paying his first visit to one of our famous public schools. After a thorough inspection of all that was going on he was asked by the headmaster to give his impressions. His answer was, I think, somewhat unexpected : " What has impressed me most", he said, "is the deplorable physique of the boys." I was not told his impression of the masters' physique, and perhaps it would have been indiscreet to inquire.

What did he mean? Not, I gather, that the boys looked diseased, or unhealthy in the animal sense, or deficient in size and muscular development. He meant that their bodies showed signs of being untrained and undisciplined in the management of their normal movements and attitudes as they walked and ran and stood about. Their bodily movements seemed to him incoherent, disorderly, muddled, awkward, ugly, wasteful, abandoned to a general condition of do-it-anyhow and go-as-you-please—uneducated bodies from his point of view. He was judging the physique of the boys by the standard of economy in movement—a standard which differs considerably from that of the physician or the athletic trainer, but is now very widely adopted by the new physical training as it is practised on the continent. He was struck, for example, by the fact that most of the boys had their hands in their pockets and, though he would doubtless have agreed with Charles Lamb that one's hands are better in one's own pocket than in one's neighbour's, he took the habit to mean that the boys were ignorant of what to do with their hands, that they found them a nuisance, were rather ashamed of them and hid them in their pockets accordingly. It was on grounds such as these—and there were many of them—that he pronounced the physique of these well-fed boys in that famous school to be deplorable.

Another testimony to the same effect comes from remarks made to me by the headmaster of a large elementary school of boys and girls in the east of London. "In this school", he said, "70 per cent. of the children have physical defects, most of which would be easily remedied by the right sort of physical culture. And a still larger percentage are what you might call physical illiterates. Not more than 5 per cent. of the children know how to stand, to sit, to walk, to run, to speak, or to breathe." That is what he meant by physical illiteracy, and I think you will agree that the condition is by no means confined to children in elementary schools. Anyone who studies a modern crowd—say the crowd at a Test Match or a race meeting—will see that physical illiteracy is an appallingly common condition in our urban populations. And if he reflects on the matter I think he will come to the conclusion that physical illiteracy, whether in a child or an adult, is bound to react unfavourably both on mental and moral development. There is something strange, to my mind, something out of proportion, in the immense efforts education has made to overcome illiteracy in the ordinary sense and the little that has been done to overcome it in the physical sense. I count it one of the most distressing phenomena of our urban civilisation.

If you ask me for a more exact definition of physical illiteracy—which of course is only a figure of speech—I would say that a physical illiterate is one who is in the same state physically that he would be mentally if he had never learned to read and write—illiterate in the ordinary sense. The analogy cannot of course be worked out in detail, but I think we may say that just as a mental illiterate is cut off from a world of knowledge by his inability to read, so the physical illiterate is cut off from a world of skill by the undisciplined condition of his body. I regard a trained body—trained to be master of its movements as a whole and not in fragments—as the necessary foundation for all kinds of creative activity, just as reading and writing are the necessary foundation for the acquisition of knowledge. And this applies not only to creativeness in the manual arts, but to the higher creativeness of thought, imagination, and morality. If we can imagine the physical culture of the community raised to the same level as its mental cultures—as it seems to have been among the Greeks—I should expect from it a marked liberation of skill in every direction—not only in the arts, though certainly in them, but in the good life generally, which is much more an affair of skill than some of our moralists realise. These muddled lives that so many of us seem to be living nowadays, muddled mentally, muddled morally, with their reflection in what is known as "world chaos"—is it fantastic to suggest that much of this originates in a muddled condition of the body, in physical illiteracy, in the lack of the intelligent and skilful control of our movements which a right physical culture would have given us? I am not so rash as to say that physical culture would turn everybody into a good citizen. But I am sure that it would give him a better chance of becoming one. It would give him more control over himself, more balance, more consistency than the average individual now has, and that would be found an immense advantage when it came to co-operating with his fellows in carrying out concerted operations for the common good. Is it not a fact that self-control, which is the basis of all the social virtues, begins by acquiring an intelligent control over the normal movements of the human body? Which is precisely what a right physical culture would aim at. That, rather than reading and writing, I regard as the true elementary education of every human being. Not that I would suppress reading and writing: they should be retained; but their value, and the value of all they lead to, even of the highest scholarship, would be increased beyond all imagining if this other thing went with them.

You will naturally ask for information as to the form which physical culture takes when the effort is made to co-ordinate it with the culture of the mind. I speak only of its underlying principles. Essentially it is a discipline of movement, founded on a scientific technique and raised to something of the dignity and beauty of an art, an art, moreover, for which the body is naturally adapted and to which it soon learns to respond. The movements practised are not merely the movements of the individual body: they extend to larger concerted operations in which the individual moves to pattern with a multitude of others like the choric dances of the Greeks; for it is an interesting fact, which I have no time to enlarge upon, that the human body is adapted, not only for harmonious movement on its own accord, but for co-operative movement on a large scale—the physical basis of human co-operation which is often talked about as though it were an affair of disembodied spirits, as it certainly is not. Man is a social being in his body as well as in his mind. Why else was he given the faculty of speech and a physical organ to emit it?

But in what, you will say, does this differ from military drill? It differs in this—that in place of a series of mechanical movements, interrupted by halts and sudden changes, the movement is now continuous and rhythmical, the response being given not to a sudden word of command but to a pattern, a rhythm, sometimes to an actual theme in music, an art to which the natural movements of the body are closely related. That is the point where the new physical culture, which is founded on the nature of the body, comes into contact with the nature of the mind, where in fact the two function as a unity. For the mind is also a *moving thing*—you might even call it movement pure and simple, its powers of concentration being at their highest when it moves in its natural rhythm (the rhythm of reason as Plato called it) which some believe is the rhythm of the universe itself. This may account for a fact reported to me by an eminent schoolmaster who had introduced the new system of physical training into his school. He reported a distinct improvement in the Latin prose—the contrary effect to that produced in my own schooldays by the cross-country runs.

In conclusion, then, it is my belief that the next great step forward in human education will be in the direction of integrating the education of the body with the education of the mind, bringing the two to the same level of dignity and importance, and making education of that kind accessible to everybody. The schoolmaster of the future will understand how it can be done and will himself have been trained to do it.

MODERN LANGUAGES AND
INTERNATIONALISM

H. J. Chaytor

INTERNATIONALISM, whatever the meaning of the term or
the purpose of the movement which the term denotes, is
ultimately dependent upon the possibility of the communication of ideas between different nationalities. The greatest
obstacle to such communication is diversity of language. It
might be thought that this barrier is being steadily broken
down; never in the world's history have the possibilities of
intercommunication by land, by sea, and by air been greater or
more rapid and easy than they are to-day; yet the paradoxical
fact confronts us, that the linguistic obstacles to communication are to-day more formidable than at any previous period
in the history of Western Europe. The contrast between the
past and the present in this respect is striking and significant.

In the ancient and mediaeval world, language was never a
bone of political contention. Under the Roman Empire, the
use and the spread of Greek was unrestricted. Cicero could
address the Syracusan senate in Greek; Greek inscriptions of
the seventh century A.D. have been found so near to Rome as
Naples, and the debt of Christianity to the κοινή, the vernacular of the Levant, is beyond calculation. The same may be
said of other languages; *in Tibrim defluxit Orontes*, without let
or hindrance. Nor did the Romans make any attempt to
impose their Latin upon subject races by the suppression of
vernacular tongues. Celtic and Iberian died out and were
supplanted by Latin in Gaul and Spain, not merely because
Latin was the official and legal language, but because it was the
language of a higher and more attractive civilisation. Spanish
tribesmen were eager to be Latinised; Sertorius set up a Latin
school for young Spanish nobles at Huesca about 80 B.C. and

the long list of eminent writers and administrators of Spanish and Celtic extraction which succeeding centuries can show is sufficient evidence of the readiness with which these peoples accepted Roman culture. In the Middle Ages, the sense of universalism, the acceptance of the Empire, of the Catholic Church and of Latin as its official language outweighed any sense of national feeling that might have inspired respect for a vernacular. Walter von der Vogelweide thinks more of the Roman Empire than of Germanism. There was the further general feeling that the end of all things was at hand, that life here was transitory and unimportant in comparison with the life to come, and the idea of progress, in our sense of the term, was hardly apprehended. Men were thus content to communicate their ideas by the most convenient means at their disposal; nor were they bound by the conventions of the printed word and the whole psychological attitude towards language which printing implies. Languages were easily learned, for no stress was laid upon a general standard of correctness, which was measured only by ability to understand and be understood. In 1356 a bishop's visitation in Cornwall was conducted in English, French, and Cornish; in the same year, one Raoul de Tremur who was excommunicated for heresy, is said to have been "lingua quadruplici latina, gallica, anglica et cornabecaque et britannica garrulus et disertus". There is no evidence of any desire or attempt, after the Norman conquest, to Gallicise the population of this country; the official enthronement of French was a matter of convenience rather than of policy and English continued to develop without serious interruption.

Naturally, when a language became a literary medium, ideas of correctness and elegance were propounded and a definite *Sprachgefühl* developed. Cicero criticises the poets of Córdoba for a Latinity displaying "pingue quoddam ac peregrinum"; Catullus satirises slovenly pronunciation; grammarians codified usage and laid down laws. When the vernaculars became literary, the same tendency is obvious;

the eleventh-century troubadours anticipate the later disputes about preciosity; Anglo-Norman writers apologise for the defective character of their French, or, like Guernes de Pont-Sainte-Maxence in his life of St Thomas the Martyr, assure us that their language is correct;

"Mis langages est bons, car en France fui nez."

Robert of Gretham in the *Miroir dez Domees*, about 1250

"Si rien i ad a amender
U del fraunceis u del rimer,
Nel teneis pas a mesprisoun,
Mes bien gardez le raisoun."

In other words, as long as the sense is understood, the French is of minor importance. Writers abandon their own language and prefer to use another for special reasons. Alfonso X, a Castilian, wrote his *Cantigas* in the thirteenth century in the Galician dialect, as the conventions of the time had appropriated this dialect as the medium for lyric poetry. Brunetto Latini in the thirteenth century wrote his *Tresor* in French instead of Italian for the reason that in his opinion "La parleure française est plus delitable et plus commune à toutes gens", and a similar reason for the same procedure is given by the chronicler Martino da Canale: "la langue française cort parmi le monde et est plus delitable à lire et à oir que nule autre." There are cases, indeed, where the use of a particular language is prescribed; in 1290 the statutes of the general chapter of the province of York ordered the members of the chapter to speak French or Latin and to avoid English;

"et quia videtur utile et honestum, qui se garritui Anglico assuescunt et ad magnates sepius pro domus sue negotiis diriguntur, ne pro defectu boni ydiomatis incidant in ruborem, statutum est ut omnes in capitulo, in proclamationibus, correcionibus, colloquiis, parlamentis, solaciis ac locis aliis colloquantur Gallicum seu Latinum; qui autem secus fecerit, in capitulo publice proclametur, et secundum meritum puniatur."

In such cases, restriction is due to social or diplomatic requirements; political considerations do not enter into the question.
The distribution of German still shows some traces of this
stage of development. German has never had a definite
linguistic boundary; it is spoken in Switzerland, Austria,
Hungary, Poland, and Russia, because the mediaeval German
was more concerned with the maintenance of the· Holy
Roman Empire than with the idea of his own nationality; so
also Frederick the Great, a thorough German at heart, pre-
ferred to speak and write French and was apparently unconscious of any disloyalty or inconsistency in his preference.

But long before Frederick's time, unity of language, like
unity of belief, had assumed a political significance. The first
step in this direction was taken by Italy, which as a whole had
never displayed any great enthusiasm for the Holy Roman
Empire. Dante was a great exception, and the universalist
views which he propounded in the *De Monarchia* led to his
exile; but it was precisely those views which led him to
anticipate with his *De Vulgari Eloquentia* the later movement
towards linguistic nationalism. The city-states of Italy pre-
ferred republican to imperial Rome; they upheld the Latin of
Cicero, Virgil, and Horace against the Latin of the Church and
the world; the humanist and Renaissance movements soon
demanded a similar standard of purity for the Italian language.
By the sixteenth century the idea of language as a national
heritage and as an expression of national character had passed
into France and effected a footing in Spain; thenceforward
the road is plain to the statement of the schoolmaster, M.
Hamel, in Daudet's *conte*, *La Dernière Classe*; "il se mit à
nous parler de la langue française, disant que c'était la plus
belle langue du monde, la plus claire, la plus solide; qu'il
fallait la garder entre nous et ne jamais l'oublier, parce que,
quand un peuple tombe esclave, tant qu'il tient bien sa langue,
c'est comme s'il tenait la clef de sa prison." In the early days of
Romanticism, scientific attempts were begun to analyse the
history of linguistic development and to formulate its laws;

the value of dialect and *patois* was appreciated by the philologist, and interest in the linguistic past aroused reverence for languages which seemed moribund, and efforts to revive them were made. The political significance of language was speedily appreciated. In Ireland, a difficult language, said to be unsuited to the needs of modern civilisation, but possessing an interesting antiquarian literature, has been made an additional burden upon the schoolboy, because it was thought to be the symbol of a nationalist revival. The expulsion of foreign terms from German has proceeded steadily. In Spain, Catalan, Basque, and Galician are the foundations upon which claims for autonomy and political decentralisation have been based. The smaller the area involved, the more preposterous are sometimes its claims. The Basques have seriously proposed the foundation of a cultural university upon the basis of a translation of the Bible and some seventeenth-century songs; a Catalan propagandist writes a treatise upon internationalism in his own tongue, and the communist agitator who wishes to preach his international gospel in Catalonia is seriously handicapped if he cannot argue in Catalan. There are cases when antiquarian pride is the chief reason for the maintenance of a dialect; for this reason Rhoeto-Romanisch holds out against German and Italian; the Provençal revival under the influence of Mistral and his school had no political significance. But in general we have arrived at a state of things inconceivable in the Middle Ages; wars are waged about language, prohibitions of language are issued, suppressions of language are practised. The late mediaeval dictum, "cujus regio, ejus religio", must now be rewritten, "cujus regio, ejus lingua". Italy takes over Southern Tyrol and proceeds to rename the localities, to enforce Italian teaching in every school and to repress German wherever possible. Utterly different was the procedure of ancient Rome, in such a case as this.

Linguistic barriers at the present day are therefore high and formidable. The brief and superficial retrospect already given may suffice to show the nature of the change that has taken place in European ideas concerning language, and the fact that this change is the outcome of a slow course of development, for which reason it is likely rather to be intensified than to diminish. Language and nation are now regarded as inseparably connected, and this idea is strengthened by the economic nationalism at present in vogue. It is admitted that language is more than a mere means of communicating or concealing ideas; it is the expression of national spirit and individuality; a national language has a style of its own; its vocabulary is a record of historical associations; its syntax betrays an individual method of thought, into which the foreigner finds it hard to penetrate with appreciation. Some years ago, two young men happened to meet in a boarding house near Paris, where Englishmen went to learn French; these two men spoke French with adequate fluency, but for the benefit of others, and for their own, they avoided English for the greater part of their stay. But during the last two days they agreed to speak English, because they wanted to make one another's acquaintance. So opaque is the veil that a foreign language spreads between two nations. Yet from that veil they will not be parted. It might be possible to induce the League of Nations to agree upon the desirability of a universal language for Europe; but a suggestion that Europe should abandon its several languages in favour of a universal tongue would not have a moment's chance of acceptance.

The difficulty is inherent in the constitution of mankind. Every social group will develop a language of its own, which tends to differentiate itself from other languages. Within a national language there are many such groups; there is a language of the drawing-room, of the barracks, of the law court, of the workshop; and there is an instinct in any community to defend its own peculiarities against those of some other group. Every schoolmaster knows the strength and the weakness of group consciousness, which produces rivalry between forms and houses; it is a consciousness not imposed from without, nor regulated by law, nor entirely dependent upon the vigour of the individuals composing the group, but produced by a community of interests, occupations or needs, and appearing at its strongest when confronted by other groups with different interests and requirements. In such a group, language is the strongest bond of unity and the most obvious symbol of unity. Individual divergencies are detected and suppressed, and in this way the tendency of each individual to depart from the common mode of speech is corrected by the necessity of making himself understood. If the groups come in contact as members of a nation, the same necessity will maintain a sufficient community of language. The inherent tendency to differentiation is corrected by the tendency to unification, and in this way an equilibrium is established. But a group wholly isolated will speedily develop a language intelligible only to its own members. On either side of a mountain range villages of the same nationality will use terms and expressions which are peculiar to themselves. Children in one family will often invent a vocabulary for use among themselves.

The use of an artificial language has been often suggested as a means of overcoming this difficulty. But the adoption of such a language as Esperanto means the abandonment in language of everything that has a specific interest. It could and does facilitate the communication of ideas upon practical matters; but, as a means for understanding the personality of a foreigner, it is useless. When Balzac wore out his boots in tramping Paris in search of suitable names for his characters, when he declined to adopt a name that had not been used or to describe a house that was purely imaginary, on the ground that such fictitious creations had no vitality, he was not entirely mystical nor fanciful. Words have their associations, sentences their cadence, verse its rhythm which a foreigner can never fully appreciate, and which an artificial language is the least fitted to reproduce. Internationalism should have as its ideal the task of reaching the intimate springs of national character, and transmuting one national sentiment into another, a task always difficult and often impossible, especially when emotion is concerned. Those who need proof of this statement need attempt only the translation of any well-known lyric poem.

If an artificial language is useless for internationalism, in the highest sense of the term, the remaining possibility is the adoption of some living language which has proved itself suitable for international use and possesses those associations and literary interests which an artificial language cannot have. English appears to be best suited for this purpose, and, of all other languages, is more nearly in the position which Latin once held. Its grammar and syntax are of the simplest, it readily naturalises any foreign term that seems convenient, its pronunciation offers no great difficulties and multitudes of foreigners find it an easy language to learn incorrectly; lower civilisations readily adopt it as a means of communication. Its one disadvantage is a bewildering and chaotic orthography, and therefore the hopes of those who expect English to become the international language of the world are usually bound up with the nostrums of a legion of spelling reformers and their numerous recipes for bringing order out of chaos or for making chaos worse confounded.

But such a language, however widely diffused, could never be more for the majority of man than what the Civil Service Commissioners politely call an auxiliary language, one that is imperfectly known. We have to face the fact that, as the idea of internationalism has become more familiar and as the ease of communication has increased, so the barrier of language has steadily become more formidable. The reason of this paradox is far from clear, but one or two considerations may be advanced. There appear to be two conflicting ideals of State-life before the world at the present time. There is the communistic ideal of the equalitarian or totalitarian State, in which the individual is of no account except is so far as he is useful to the State and in which, therefore, economic equality of individuals is a fundamental principle; the exponents of this

ideal insist upon internationalism as their final purpose, for the
reason that the socialist or communist State will always be
defeated by capitalism in the economic field; it seems to be
generally recognised that under capitalism the costs of production are lower than under any form of socialised industrial-
ism. In short, the arguments and ideals of those who support
the equalitarian State are economic in character; they are
concerned only with life sublunary and declare that the
possibilities of a life to come have nothing to do with them.
On the other side are a number of old-established civilisations
which are fundamentally individualist in character; in their
most characteristic form, as Christian states, they consider
that the individual is the *raison d'être* of the State, that the form
of the State matters nothing, as it is but a temporary arrangement enabling mankind to live under the social conditions
necessary for his development; personal liberty and not
economic equality is their ideal. Both have something in
common; Christianity, like communism, is international,
and declares itself the champion of the poor and the oppressed;
but upon the question of the destiny and purpose of the
individual they are divided beyond any hope of conciliation.
Is it not possible that the greater insistence upon the political
significance of language which has accompanied the growth
of the international ideal may be the instinctive revolt of
individualism against a universalism which is abhorrent to its
very nature? In any case, this seems to be a question which the
equalitarians have not yet considered, though it is of immense
importance to them; for people who speak different languages
will certainly think different thoughts.

Many internationalists appear to assume that the removal of
all linguistic barriers would immediately transform European
life into one grand sweet song. The assumption is unfounded;
individual experience might suggest the opposite; most of us
can think of bores from whom we would gladly be defended
by the barrier of Basque or Mandarin Chinese, and it would be
possible to write an effective treatise under the motto, "omne

ignotum pro pacifico"; the less we know of some people the more likely we are to esteem them. A long period of education would be needed to prepare alien nationalities for unrestricted intercourse. But the most superficial knowledge of the history of linguistic developments will show that the curse or the blessing of Babel will remain with us for all time. And yet, if civilisation is to continue international contact must be made, though it will never be possible at more than a number of points which are very few in comparison with the populations involved; universal international comprehension is a possibility too remote to deserve serious consideration. It is better to ask what can be done to increase and improve such points of contact as exist.

It is hardly necessary to explain to a meeting of practical schoolmasters what has been done in the last thirty years for the improvement of modern-language teaching. Immense trouble has been taken, and with a considerable measure of success to teach languages as living means of communication, and at the same time to inspire interest in the life and spirit of other nationalities. History is no longer taught as though England were the hub of the universe; every week brings new books intended to introduce schoolboys to the institutions and manners of foreign peoples; international correspondence has grown; school journeys abroad have become common.

In the course of last year the Modern Language Association placed hundreds of boys and girls in communication with foreign correspondents and negotiated a large number of exchanges of children with those of foreign families. Such work produces a number of points of contact at which the ground has been properly prepared, and the visitors are ready to appreciate and anxious to understand. It is to be regretted that efforts of this nature are chiefly confined to relations with France and Germany; little is done for Spain, and practically nothing for Italy. Yet the peace of Europe depends upon our dealings with all four of these countries. It is much to be wished that English education could abandon the tradition that French is the first language to be studied. Great as are its claims, it has certain disadvantages; it is more difficult for the English learner than any other Romance language, except possibly Romanian, and it would be more successfully studied if it were begun at a later age than is usual. We need a greater variety of choice for the boy or girl with some linguistic capacity who is able, as many are, to study three languages at school. The difficulties of expense and organisation are obvious, but if a larger number would learn Italian and Spanish at school, we should by degrees obtain a body of well-informed people who could interpret to their own nation the culture of these countries and induce them to learn more about ourselves. In this way a general consciousness of the tasks before Western Europe will be created and ideals of policy and conduct will be formed and pursued.

An internationalism that aims at the obliteration of all national characteristics is doomed to failure. The best illustration of true internationalism can be seen in the working of our ancient universities. In these exist a number of colleges, independent corporations, managing their own affairs, with idiosyncrasies of their own, jealous of their independence, and living in a certain friendly rivalry with one another; but all united by the sense that they are members of a university, to the success of which they have each a contribution to make, and the reputation of which it is their privilege to maintain. If the five great nations of Western Europe could be brought to regard their association in a similar light the internationalist would have achieved all that he can reasonably hope to attain and all that is practically necessary. The most indispensable means to this end is a better knowledge of modern languages.

THE WRITING OF ENGLISH AT SCHOOL AND ELSEWHERE

J. Dover Wilson

Flee fro the prees and dwelle with sothfastnesse.
Geoffrey Chaucer, *Truth*.

DOUBTLESS we shall all live to see some intrepid angel—
for it's bound to be a woman—crossing the Atlantic in a
single hour; but only a fool would attempt to traverse in the
same period the vast ocean which we label English on our
scholastic charts. I am going, therefore, to confine myself to
one bay of the subject—a bay in exploring which a term might
easily be spent—I mean the writing of English, or rather the
writing of English by boys under magisterial stimulus and
correction.

I have chosen this arm of our great sea for several reasons.
First, I am addressing an audience of teachers professing many
subjects. Only a proportion of us are what are called "English
specialists"—an expression I sometimes wish had never been
invented. Yet every one in this room, I suppose, at one time
or other—often at many times—has to teach English. In the
words of the famous report on *The Teaching of English in
England*: "The teaching of English as the instrument of
thought and the means of communication will necessarily
affect the teaching of every other subject. Whatever view is
taken of specialisation in schools, it is evidently desirable that
the general education of every teacher shall be sufficiently
good to ensure unceasing instruction in the English language.
The teachers of all special subjects must be responsible for
the quality of the English spoken and written during their
lessons. In every department of school work confused and
slovenly English must be regarded as the result of a failure on

the part of the teacher".* The old constitutional maxim, which lies at the root of our parliamentary institutions, that what touches all should be considered by all, implies an obligation as well as a right; and I make no apology for speaking about English speech in this little parliament of English public schoolmasters. Indeed, I can hardly help myself; for the longer I live and have to do with university graduate students, to say nothing of other so-called educated persons, the more urgently this problem of written English forces itself upon my attention. You are concerned with the teaching of many subjects to boys through the medium of the mother tongue. I am concerned with honours graduates in many subjects, and in the mother tongue I often find them woefully deficient.

A professor of education is the head of a department for the training of teachers; at King's, for the training of teachers in secondary schools. "Training" suggests presumptuous claims, and I should like to substitute the word "initiation" did not that in turn suggest freemasonry or the Rosicrucians. An education department is really a kind of swimming bath in which the novice can learn a few strokes and gain confidence before committing himself to the deep and maybe turbulent waters of professional scholastic life. But whatever it does or attempts to do, such a department, being the meeting place of most academic subjects, offers an excellent conning-tower for the inspection of the finished products of our modern education. Every year about a hundred men and women who have just taken their degrees—first or second class honours degrees, for the most part—pass through the education department at King's, and at the end of the twelve months' course sit for the Teachers' Diploma Examination of the University of London. Furthermore I lecture to and help to examine some three hundred other students of the same type belonging to the Institute of Education and similar training departments in London, students drawn, like those

* pp. 23–4.

at King's, not only from London University but from many other universities, including those of Oxford and Cambridge. It is admirable material, the fine flower of one branch of our educational system. And one cannot help feeling cheerful about the future of secondary education, the shaping of which lies in their hands, as one contemplates the physique, the courtesy, the good humour, and the academic distinction of these hundreds of happy young people. Yet, if the ability to read and write one's own language be the minimum qualification of an educated man or woman, then not a small percentage of these highly qualified intending teachers must be set down as almost illiterate, inasmuch as they are incapable of reading anything aloud "with good accent★ and good discretion" or of expressing themselves on paper with point and coherence. There is, of course, another section the members of which speak and write well; but these, though happily numerous, form a minority of the whole.

You will perhaps be thinking that the illiterates belong to a special social stratum, that they come from "poor homes", homes without books, without the daily conversation about things of the mind which provides that impalpable but all-important element in education called "background". It is true that many students in London lack this element. Indeed, the gossip goes that at least one recently succeeded in obtaining university honours without ever having possessed a book in his life! Yet the problem is not simply an economic one. There are many large houses in the suburbs round London, houses with expensively laid out and profusely stocked gardens, but with no culture save horticulture and with no books except those of the wallpaper kind provided by enterprising publishers, for decoration not for use. Most of the boys from such homes find their way into public schools. I suspect that lack of background is as common among your

★ By "good accent" I mean, as Polonius did, right stress, not the accepted dialect of well-to-do Londoners known as Standard English.

pupils as among my students. Fifty-five years ago Matthew Arnold declared that the English upper class, "with no necessary function to fulfil, never conversant with life as it really is, tempted, flattered, spoilt from childhood to old age ...is inevitably materialised, and the more so the more the development of industry and ingenuity augments the means of luxury".* What would he say now, if he could glance at our illustrated monthlies? The Barbarians are still with us, more barbaric than ever.

We are better mannered, cleaner and healthier in body, more humane, and—assuming Mr Hore Belisha gets his way with the Barbarians in their chariots—longer lived than our forefathers. But good English is very seldom heard in the homes of to-day. In former times, the daily reading of the Bible and the Book of Common Prayer attuned the young ear to the rhythms of the best English prose ever written, enriched the young vocabulary with the simplest words for the greatest things, filled the expanding mind with countless images, images now of the utmost grandeur:

"The heavens declare the glory of God: and the firmament showeth his handiwork....

In them hath he set a tabernacle for the sun: which cometh forth as a bridegroom out of his chamber, and rejoiceth as a giant to run his course."

And now of the most engaging homeliness:

"The Lord is my shepherd: therefore can I lack nothing.

He shall feed me in the green pasture: and lead me forth beside the waters of comfort....

Yea, though I walk through the valley of the shadow of death, I will fear no evil: for thou art with me: thy rod and thy staff shall comfort me.

Thou hast prepared a table before me; thou hast anointed my head with oil, and my cup shall be full."

Thus, unconsciously, and without the aid of any pedagogue,

* *Mixed Essays*, p. 88.

the English people, like the Greeks of old, grew in grace, being nourished upon music, the music of one of the greatest literatures of the world.

You remember Plato's words:

"And therefore, Glaucon, a musical education is a more potent instrument than any other, because rhythm and harmony find their way into the inward places of the soul on which they mightily fasten, imparting grace, and making the soul of him who is rightly educated graceful... now in the days of his youth, even before he is able to know the reason why; and when reason comes he will recognise and salute the friend with whom his education has made him long familiar."

The rhythm and harmony which find their way into the secret places of the souls of the modern child are often of a different kind: they bellow from the non-selective loud-speaker, which is never turned off. It will be said that the mild blare of the wireless is a lesser evil than the bitter and exacerbating cries of rival sects, and that the sacred books were too often used as arsenals for most un-Christian hostilities. I agree. In no respect has this nation made greater and more indubitable advance in my lifetime than in the decline of religious animosity, a decline which I attribute largely to the development of popular education. The gain is great, but there is much loss too. Apart from all questions of religion, when the English people ceased to take an interest in the English Bible, they lost the traditional basis of their national culture; and no substitute has since been found.

It will be said, again, that the nation is far more literate than it ever was, that if boys and girls *hear* the English language less, they read it more. True, but what do they read? Advertisements, the captions of the picture-house, evening news-papers, and shoddy tales: catchpenny prose—full of ill-chosen words, ill-shaped sentences, cheap and ill-assorted images— the rubbish of a thousand presses which utter themselves

5-2

without thought, without conscience, without vision. Better written, perhaps, but no higher in the moral scale are the cheap morning journals: *The Daily Stunt, The Daily Whim, The Daily Sneer,* or, for sabbath reading, *The Universe of Crime,* incorporating *The Henroost of High Life,* newspapers which needs must smirch the highest when they see it, and of which the editors almost seem to have said to the scribes who serve them: Whatsoever things are true, whatsoever things are honest, whatsoever things are just, whatsoever things are pure, whatsoever things are lovely, whatsoever things are of good report: if there be any virtue, and if there be any praise, cheapen these things.★ Rousseau, who saw that in the corrupt society amid which he lived "one must set up a fence betimes round a child's soul", tells us that "at twelve years of age Émile will hardly know what a book is". It might be well if our modern Émiles were in the same blessed state as regards cheap literature until a far higher age. Yet, to many of them, what alternative is offered but so-called educational literature, the jejune, unappetising, desiccated husks of learning, the text-books, upon which youth,

★ Since this lecture was delivered the Lord Chief Justice of England, in a letter to *The Times* on the occasion of its centenary, has expressed himself on the subject of the cheap press in terms even stronger than those used above. Here are his words: "We who read *The Times* know what we get. Do we fail to recognize what we escape and avoid? It is worth while sometimes to spend a penny—I do it now and again for a particular purpose—in some one or other of many other directions in order to see what a newspaper can become in different hands. If Ruskin were alive to-day would he, or would he not, in relation to a sadly large section of the Press, be inclined to dot the i's and cross the t's of his well-known rebuke to: 'The hireling scribes of the newspaper Press who daily pawn the dirty linen of their souls for the price of a bottle of sour wine and a cigar'? What would he have to say to the infamous abyss in which 'personal journalism', as it is called, is to-day wallowing? Might he not think (as some of us do) that the time is almost ripe for legislation?".

if studious, must browse; or the pabulum of the junior class-room, too soft or too sticky to bite on, lest the children's teeth be set on edge? And are not we, the teachers of youth, responsible for the standard of modern journalism? We are now reaping the harvest sown in the Education Act of 1870 which gave us a population taught to read, but not taught to distinguish between what is good and what is bad in that which they read.

Hearing English, reading English, what of writing English? What practice in writing do most boys get in school? As far as I can judge from the finished articles which pass through my hands, often nothing—beyond the hurried answers to examination questions. Many have to be taught, as graduates, first of all to read, and next to write. Why? Because they have never before had time to do either—they have been *working*, first for county scholarships, then for "matric.", then for "inter", and lastly for that crown of earthly glory, the final examination of the Honours School; their vision, their leisure, their opportunities for reading and for writing, growing narrower at each step. What shall it profit a man, if he gain a first class and lose his own soul?

A large number of the young men and women leaving our universities, old and new, are not really educated at all: that is to say, they have never learned to think independently or to appreciate spontaneously. Crammed with mere facts and with the half-understood opinions or phrases of other people, they have grown accustomed to accept these passively instead of trying to form opinions of their own. They have, therefore, tended to lose not merely all interest in the objects or ideas which are the stuff of educated thought, but even the very capacity to think consecutively. Our modern premature specialisation is the latest and the greatest enemy of true education.

This specialisation is due to an anarchy of the school curriculum nearly as serious as the anarchy of taste, aesthetic and moral, we have just been considering. Almost within a single generation the nation has suffered a double disaster: it has lost the traditional basis of its culture by its neglect of the Authorised Version, and it has lost the traditional centre of its school curriculum by its surrender of the classics. I am not here to plead for the classics. They will never resume their ancient sovereignty; and their obvious, their only possible successor, is the English language. Yet so far English is no more than one of many competing subjects in the school; and that partly because it has not yet proved its title to reign. The technique of English teaching, especially the teaching of English speech and writing, has still to be worked out. Great progress has been made; new advances are registered every year; but we are not yet in sight of anything like finality in our methods, still less of general consent for them. There is much to do before the teaching of English holds a position comparable with that held by the teaching of French in France or with that held by the teaching of Latin in England fifty years ago.

Here, I think, the public schools can give a lead to the other schools of England, as they have often done in the past; not merely because of their prestige, but because, the classical tradition being still strong in them, though it weakens every day, they seem best fitted to effect the carry-over from the one sovereignty to the other.

English, especially the writing of English prose, must become the central and essential subject of the school curriculum, a subject to which every teacher will give heed but which will run throughout the school course as the special concern of certain men whom I would call not "English specialists", but form masters. It must take the place of Latin, and must perform the function that Latin has for centuries performed; it must make our citizens into good rhetoricians, to use Quintilian's term; teach them, that is, to *think* and to express their thoughts.

We need a New Rhetoric, which will be what the Old Rhetoric was to the Greeks, the Romans, and the men of the

Renaissance; a training in speech, not through the medium of a foreign language, but through the mother tongue itself. I shall be told that the mother tongue is too familiar, too rich, too vague, or what not, to serve as such an instrument. I reply that if the language of Homer and Aeschylus was not too familiar or too rich for the discipline of the boys of Athens, the language of Bacon and Shakespeare, Milton and Burke, ought to be adequate for the boys of England. That it seems *not* to be so is because we have either neglected to give our mind to the matter or have misapprehended it. I appeal to you teachers of the public schools to give your minds to it, to consider with yourselves how best you can help the nation at this crisis in the history of its culture. You have ampler occasions of leisure than your colleagues of the day schools; you are the heirs of a great tradition; some of the very best brains in the country are under your care, the industrial and political leaders of the next generation. I need not remind you of your responsibilities; you are conscious enough of these, I do not doubt. Have you appreciated to the same extent your opportunities? I believe that well-considered experiments in the teaching of the mother tongue carried on in the public schools to-day might prove of the very greatest national value.

Give it then your mind; but do not misapprehend! The New Rhetoric must attain all the ends of the Old Rhetoric— I am optimistic enough to think its achievement will be much greater—without a slavish imitation which will defeat those very ends themselves. There can be no doubt that progress in the teaching of English in this country has been much hindered by unintelligent adoption of methods suitable to the teaching of Latin. This is especially so in regard to what is called English Grammar. Let me say three things upon this vexed subject:

(1) Directly a boy is old enough to think about his language and to discuss it with his elders, a certain amount of grammatical knowledge is necessary—otherwise he will have no

names for the different parts of speech, the different functions of language, and will therefore be incapable of thinking or talking about the matter at all. I will not say that the couplet in *Hudibras*—

> For all a rhetorician's rules
> Teach nothing but to name his tools—

contains the whole truth—but it sets us on the right road. Grammar is a purely utilitarian subject: it gives us an agreed nomenclature, a number of convenient labels for use in handling language—that is all. It does not in itself help us much to write or speak the language better—which brings me to my second point:

(2) There is little relation between grammatical knowledge and a command of English. Dr Ballard, the well-known L.C.C. inspector and at the same time an excellent psychologist, has shown in his *Teaching the Mother Tongue* that

(*a*) composition in "a grammar-ridden school" is often inferior to that in a grammarless school, and that it improves in the same school when the teaching of grammar is discontinued, and that

(*b*) children who are "good at grammar" are by no means necessarily good at composition, and *vice versa*.

The idea that we learn "correct" English by learning English grammar is one of the illusions bequeathed to us by the classical tradition. For an English boy grammar is an indispensable means of approach to Latin—though, as Dr Rouse of the Perse School has shown, it is less indispensable than is usually supposed—because Latin is a foreign language, and the readiest way to learn a foreign language, if you are unable to visit the country where it is spoken, is to master its skeleton outline. On the other hand, the English boy has long spoken English before he comes to school; he needs to improve and enrich something he already possesses; and this is to be done by practice under expert guidance, by imitating good models, and by reading widely—not by parsing and analysis. But we have inherited another, and still worse, illusion from the Renaissance, viz. that English grammar is a sort of poor relation to Latin grammar. In other words,

(3) A great deal of what now passes as English grammar in school text-books is nothing of the kind.

The grammar of modern English is only in our own day being worked out by students of language like Otto Jespersen; and, until their task is accomplished, he is a bold man who would take upon him to lay down the law. Open Jespersen's *Essentials of English Grammar* and your eye lights on strange terms and unaccustomed notions, such as primaries, secondaries and tertiaries, adjuncts and adnexes; and you realise that here is a great linguist, perhaps the greatest linguist alive, sitting down before the structure of our language and thinking it all out afresh, from the beginning. The old categories and terms do not fit, because they were in the main borrowed from Latin grammar; and two languages could hardly be more different than English and Latin. English is extremely analytical; after Chinese, perhaps the most analytical speech yet devised by man. Latin is highly synthetic. Compare "cantavisset" with its equivalent "he might have sung" and you get a measure of the difference: the one a "solidity and compound mass", the other four detachable words (like railway-trucks or the spare parts of a modern machine) which can be used in all sorts of other connexions and combinations. Obviously the grammars of such diverse tongues must be themselves diverse; yet most so-called "English grammar-books" are constructed on the analogy of Latin. It follows that English grammar is an exceedingly difficult and dangerous subject to handle in the class-room; and though I have, I suppose, heard scores of lessons upon it, I do not remember finding myself in complete agreement with a single one of them. This does not mean that the names of the principal tools cannot be taught: functions like the substantive, the adjective, the adverb, the verb, person and number are common to most languages. It is when one ventures out of this narrow territory, e.g. into questions of case, of declension, and of conjugation, that one finds oneself on boggy soil. Idiomatic usage again is particularly treacherous; and there are many forms of speech, sanctioned by antiquity and supported by great authority, which are now often condemned by ignorant "grammarians".

An amusing example came to my hand as I was preparing the notes for this address. Mr P. A. Barnett, formerly chief inspector of training colleges under the Board of Education and a man whose name is deservedly a household word in educational circles, has recently enlivened the tedium of retirement—if tedium can cast its shadow upon so vivacious and resourceful a mind—by preparing for the press a little book entitled *Common-Sense Grammar*. It is the shortest grammar I know, and for that reason among others one of the best for school purposes. Yet, even within the compass of forty-six small pages, its author trips more than once; so beset "with pitfall and with gin" is the road that grammarians must tread. For instance, under the heading "Common Errors" at the end of the book, I find this dictum: "*Different* should be followed by *from*, though people who should know better sometimes say *to*". Unhappily one of the persons here condemned is none other than H. W. Fowler himself whose article on "different" in *Modern English Usage* begins thus roundly: "That *different* can only be followed by *from* and not by *to* is a SUPERSTITION". Among many other bogies from which the exorcist Fowler has delivered us is the split infinitive. You will recollect his five-fold classification: "The English-speaking world may be divided into (1) those who neither know nor care what a split infinitive is; (2) those who do not know, but care very much; (3) those who know and condemn; (4) those who know and approve; and (5) those who know and distinguish". *Modern English Usage* is not yet ten years old, and is still unknown to many teachers of English. But it is the greatest contribution to clear and sensible thinking about our speech since the appearance of

Dr Johnson's *Dictionary*, and promises to exert as permanent an influence; to become, as a contemporary Frenchman declared Johnson did, "en quelque sorte une Académie pour son île". With Fowler at our elbow, a large number of our doubts are resolved, and even when a point is left undecided, it is presented to us in all its aspects with such luminous (and humorous) clarity that nothing remains to say or do, except make our choice.

The common faults, however, of ill-educated or immature writers are not usually grammatical errors, or even the kind of confusion with which Fowler deals, but rather faults due to poverty of vocabulary, bad taste, muddle-headedness, smudgy imagery, and general lack of attention; in a word, what Newman called that "haziness of intellectual vision" which is "the malady of all classes of men by nature". The most obvious effect of such haziness or laziness (the two mental states are intimately connected) is an inaccurate use of words. And here "the old classical grind" undoubtedly acted as a corrective by insisting all the time, whether in translation or in the writing of "proses", upon the importance of seeking for the right word, and by setting up, in this way, habits of intellectual integrity in the use of language. But I do not need to remind you that the teacher has all sorts of means at his disposal of encouraging habits of this kind without resorting to the classics. He can get his boys to play about with "synonyms" and "antonyms", if only to show them that such categories may hardly be said to exist. He can practise them in the use of that essential instrument of the writer's craft, the dictionary. Every time, again, the circle of knowledge and experience is widened by lessons in class, his pupils are given fresh words or phrases to express their new thoughts, words and phrases which cannot be too carefully chosen or too clearly explained. How many teachers of history realise, for example, that one of their chief functions is to introduce pupils to the political vocabulary of England, which means laying the foundation of the political thought of the rising generation? And the vocabularies of geography, of science, of mathematics, of literary criticism are scarcely less important. With the vocabulary of linguistics I have already dealt: we call it grammar. Every subject in the curriculum, every side of life, has its grammar; and the naming of the tools is an essential aid to their skilful handling.

The trouble is, as I have said, that we live in a world of shoddy work, in which the journeymen of language are constantly mishandling and misnaming the tools. Those who till the garden of the classics, "fenced from passion and mishap" because it is the garden of the Sleeping Beauty where nothing changes and not a breath of life stirs, have a simple task compared with the guardianship and transmission of a living language. The English master has not only to inculcate good habits but to be ever trying to counteract the infection of bad ones. One form of the inaccurate use of words is that called Jargon, the slip-shod speech which we read in almost every newspaper and from which it is well-nigh impossible to protect ourselves, still less our pupils. When the eye lights upon expressions like "centre round" (centre in), "phenomenal" (unusual), "transpire" (happen), "emphatically" (undoubtedly), or "somewhat unique" (rather remarkable) several times a day, how can one keep one's own speech unspotted from the world? Still more catching is the trick of pretentiousness which gives us, for instance, "the individual in question" for "this person", "constitutes a leading feature" for "is conspicuous" or "he was conveyed to his place of residence in an intoxicated condition" for "he was carried home drunk".

The last beautiful example comes from Q's "Interlude on Jargon" in *The Art of Writing* and illustrates what he condemns as one of the chief vices of modern English prose, the love of abstractions. Phrases like "in connexion with", "in respect of", "the necessity for", "the intention of", "in the direction of", "in consequence of", "the question of", "in pursuance of", provide the scaffolding to a great deal of printed English to-day. They are not wrong in themselves; but when they follow each other, sentence after sentence, like the "butterwomen's rank to market", they become infinitely tiresome, and are perhaps the principal foe of life and interest in what is written for our learning or instruction in this age. Our dislike of the concrete, our avoidance of verbs and of the subordinate sentence, have something in them more than natural if philosophy could find it out. Townsend Warner, an honoured name within these walks, counselled well when he bade his boys "be on the watch for abstract nouns and kill many of them. You can generally use verbs or adjectives in their place.... You will find them clinging to your pen like the long hairs in the post-office ink. Clean them out". Post-office ink gives philosophy a clue; for abstractions are part of official jargon, which with the modern growth of government activity, no doubt a necessary growth in itself, becomes more and more our daily bread. Got by timidity on journalese— such is their parentage, timidity which shuns the direct and the actual to avoid offence or to conceal ignorance. Abstract and circumlocutory phrases commit a man less than good forthright English; that is one reason why the journalist and the official love them. Note, for instance, the common use of "as" in government documents. An ordinary mortal will speak of "the relation between two departments"; a member of such departments speaks of "the relation *as* between" them. The difference is subtle, but not unimportant. Or take the following preamble to Circular 1294, with which the Board of Education greeted the publication of the report on *The Teaching of English* in 1921:

"The Board have had under consideration the highly important and valuable recommendations contained in the reports of the Committees which were appointed to consider the positions of Natural Science, Modern Languages, Classics and English in the educational system of this country. If the Board have hitherto refrained from expressing any opinion upon the recommendations contained in these reports, it has been through no lack of appreciation, but because they considered it desirable to wait until they were in a position to consider the recommendations of the various reports, not only separately, but also in their relation to each other. It is only since the publication of the English report that this consideration has become possible."

There is nothing *wrong* with this, except that it is quite dead. All might have been said in a single sentence; and the poverty of the mind (or minds, for the Board is plural) behind it may be gauged from the occurrence of "consider" or "consideration" five times and of "recommendations contained in these reports" three times in less than a dozen lines. If gold ruste, what shal iren do?

Much has been written upon jargon of recent years: first, I think, by Dr R. W. Chapman of the Oxford University Press, whose little book *The Portrait of a Scholar*, containing an essay on "The Decay of Syntax", is too little known in teaching circles; then by Q, in the lecture referred to above, which owes some debt to Dr Chapman; and lastly, following Q in turn, by Townsend Warner whose joyous book *On the Writing of English* should render for ever immune the boy that has read it to the poison which

barks about
Most lazar-like with vile and loathsome crust

the native simplicity of our English tongue.

I have already quoted Townsend Warner once; but his whole book is worth quotation, so that I do not apologise for borrowing from it again. He has an admirable chapter headed "On 'Succulent Bivalves'", by which he means clichés, or, as Dr Johnson called them, clenches, the stereotyped phrases, the mouldy out-worn expressions or hackneyed quotations, the reach-me-downs of hasty thought. Many people never "write", they "commit words to paper"; never "arrive", they "reach their appointed destination"; never "beg", they "put forth earnest solicitations"; never come up, as Englishmen speaking by the clock used to do, "in the nick of time", they "appear at the psychological moment", the meaning of which no man knows; never "sleep soundly", they "sleep the sleep of the just"; and when they ask their friends to keep a secret, they bid them "tell it not in Gath". The generation that has given up reading its Bible still retains some poor fragments of it in the rag-bag of its style; but how are the mighty fallen, and the weapons of war perished, when David's lament for Saul and Jonathan comes to such an end! "Have you ever seen an old bone lying in the road?" asks Townsend Warner. "Watch and you will see every dog that comes along run to it, smell it, pick it up, chew it for a moment, and then drop it for the next comer. Well, that muddy, mumbled bone is your 'ready-made phrase'—your 'succulent bivalve'. 'Is thy servant a dog that he should do this thing?'" Yet how can one learn to avoid the rags and the bones without a sense of values in language, and how is this sense to be had except by reading much good English and by being made aware of what is shoddy in bad English? I have little doubt that Townsend Warner himself made a black list of such iniquities, and taught his boys to fear them like the plague.

Then there is metaphor. Most of my university students come to grief through blurred imagery, and I very rarely find any of them who have had instruction in this matter at school. Yet surely nothing is easier than to awaken first a boy's consciousness, and then his conscience, about metaphor. My graduate writers seem to be quite unaware that a metaphor calls up a picture or that by combining two incongruous pictures they may fall into great absurdity. Had they but once read Fowler's amusing and exhaustive article on the subject in *Modern English Usage*, they might write with new eyes; for one writes with the eye as well as with the pen. What they lack is not brains, but instruction. Here, as elsewhere,

> The hungry sheep look up, and are not fed,
> But, swoln with wind and the rank mist they draw,
> Rot inwardly, and foul contagion spread.

I have dwelt thus long upon the use of words because that is where the teacher must begin, and success here will carry him some way. Not, of course, all the way; it has not even brought us to what may rightly be called composition. The hour's flight—or shall I call it flyting?—is nearly over, and we have hardly as yet caught a view of the bay as a whole. There is time for a sentence or two more only. The first shall be quoted from Thomas Wilson's *Arte of Rhetorique*, 1553. "Composition", he writes, "is an apte ioyning together of wordes in such an order that neither the eare shall espie any iarre, nor yet any man shalbe dulled with over-long drawing out of a sentence." It would be difficult to add anything to this admirable statement. I will only ask you to consider its bearing upon what Dr R. W. Chapman, in the article already mentioned, calls "the general paralysis of structure which deforms almost all modern writing", and to compare it with his blunt conclusion that "in general the modern sentence has neither rhythm nor structure; it goes on till it drops". I do not suggest that we ought to return to the formal and rigid style of the eighteenth century, but I am sure that it would do boys no harm to play the sedulous ape for a time to Burke and Gibbon, to Addison and even to Dr Johnson. Such exercises in imitation would at least teach them that the sentence and the paragraph should possess shape and proportion. The principles of all the arts bear a close resemblance, and what Ruskin wrote about architecture may well stand as a text for those learning—which of us is not?— to write English.

"Wherever Proportion exists at all, one member of the composition must be either larger than, or in some way supreme over, the rest. There is no proportion between equal things. They can have symmetry only, and symmetry without proportion is not composition.... Any succession of equal things is agreeable; but to compose is to arrange unequal things, and the first thing to be done in beginning a composition is to determine which is to be the principal thing.

I believe that all that has been written and taught about proportion, put together, is not to the architect worth the single rule, well enforced: 'Have one large thing and several smaller things, or one principal thing and several inferior things, and bind them well together'."*

I have intentionally spent most of my hour in attempting to diagnose the disease, a disease which I think threatens the very life of the English people. We can canvass remedies in the discussion to follow. Indeed, that is what I am here for: to learn from you what you are doing about it all, and what I can do to help you. After all, the main remedy for our discontents is clear, which does not mean that it is easy. All teachers in secondary schools, whether "public" or "municipal", should become aware of the evil and refuse to tolerate it; all, in short, should regard themselves, and train themselves, as above everything guardians of the purity of our speech, whatever their own special subject may be. We lead the world in the athletics of the body; let us now look to the athletics of the mind. The responsibility rests upon the whole staff; but I think that a special responsibility belongs to the form master, whom I should like to see restored to his former dignity as the keeper of the boy's intellectual conscience. I do not wish him, as I have said before, necessarily to be an English specialist. On the contrary, a good classics, history, or modern language master would probably do the job as well, if not better. But he must be specially interested in, and specially qualified for, the teaching of English composition, upon which the form, in my judgment, should spend at least two whole periods a week.

May I, in conclusion, suggest one or two principles for the planning of such courses in the writing of English?

First, the course should be progressive, i.e. the exercises should increase in difficulty as the course proceeds. Without this, composition lacks an interest which belongs to practically

---

* *Seven Lamps of Architecture*. "Beauty", xxv–xxvi.

every other subject in the curriculum, the interest of "getting on", of pressing forward from point to point or even (at the lowest) from page to page. The course, therefore, should aim at covering a definite field each year, perhaps each term. Lack of aim means loss of time, and both master and pupil will benefit from setting their face towards a goal, even if they never reach it. Some day a specific standard of proficiency in the writing of English may be expected and exacted of every boy or girl, whether literary or scientific, before promotion from one form to another. We are far from this at present; but the first step is the planning out of courses in composition.

All this has some bearing upon the difficult question of Correction. A master who sets exercises for his pupils to write, in accordance with the gradual development of their powers, should have far less to correct than the old-fashioned teacher who gives them a subject like "Spring" and lets them sprawl all over the place. The pupils' task ought not to be much, if at all, beyond their power to execute well, especially if aim be to develop the capacity of performing it in a workmanlike manner. Apprentices in cabinet-making or engineering are not asked to accomplish impossible pieces of work, partly because the material is valuable, but partly because experience has taught the craftsman that he can only learn a little at a time. Furthermore, if the theme or the exercise be only just ahead of the class, the boys will be competent, with slight assistance, to correct each other's work.

The exercises should not only be graded according to difficulty but should vary in type. The old form of composition tended to be very monotonous, and even to-day composition is still too often the writing of an essay upon a set theme. I am not one of those who would rule the essay out; it does very well in the sixth form. But it is a difficult kind of writing and should only occasionally be attempted in middle forms. There is so much else to do! There are exercises in different vocabulary-groups, e.g. the vocabulary of the home, the street, the sea, the country-side, of sport and hobbies, of history, geography, literature, science, of politics and economics, of the office, the workshop, of engineering and aircraft—the number of verbal arenas in which our colts may learn their paces is almost endless. Then there is variety of treatment. A class, for instance, may be asked to write narrative, description, argument, exposition, explanation, expansion, summary, note-taking, précis, letters, sketches, dialogues, playlets, verse translation (e.g. out of dialect into standard English, or the modernisation of antique prose), newspaper reports (e.g. of a class debate, of some historical scene, or of a school match), general knowledge papers, and so on.

Lastly, while on the subject of variety of treatment, I should like to draw what seems to me an important distinction, that between Statement and Expression. The speaking or writing of the mother tongue may be looked at from two points of view. We may think of it as the utterance of a personality, his thoughts or his dreams; and this I call Expression, the highest type of which is poetry. Or we may think of it as the representation of objective facts or impersonal concepts; and this I call Statement, the highest type of which is the language of science or philosophy. However personal or however objective, most things written or spoken contain both elements, though in varying proportions. Between, let us say, a lyric of Shelley's and a proposition in Euclid, the one a supreme example of self-expression and the other an illustration of statement as nearly impersonal as anything human, short of bare mathematical formulae, can be, there lies a whole scale of possible combinations. The distinction is relative rather than absolute; but it is vital, since it connotes a distinction of aim and in some degree of method. We need exercises in both types from our pupils; but the traditional form of composition in class is usually a test in expression, whereas exercises in statement should surely predominate in the middle forms of the school, both because they are harder and because they are an invaluable discipline for the adolescent mind. I am not here committing the well-known psychological fallacy known as the "doctrine of formal training". There is one subject, and perhaps only one, in the curriculum which is and must be a discipline for the mind; and that is the thinking with pen and ink which we call composition.

For, once again, we write to express thoughts and ideas, not to "commit words to paper". And a writer has only one source for these thoughts and ideas—himself: the style is the man. His writing will be good according to its sincerity and its grip. If it be full of echoes from other people or of mouldy commonplaces from the pavement or the market-place, it will be bad. If, on the other hand, it be mechanical, a writing that constantly falls into empty and meaningless phrases, because the writer is lazy or hurried, and lets his pen run on like a machine out of control, it will be equally bad. "Style is the ultimate morality of mind." If then the writer will improve his writing, he must begin by improving himself. He can do this in two ways: by enriching his personality and by disciplining it. He can enrich his personality by studying the writings of those who have written supremely well, especially of the great poets and thinkers. He can discipline his personality by practising English as an art or craft; an art, like other arts, involving concentration of thought, careful selection, and a thorough mastery of material. Through such practice the efficiency of his mind will be increased. It will become more lucid in its conceptions, more exact in its discriminations, richer in idea, readier in utterance, and finally more fastidious in its taste, until it comes to hate the half-thought which gives birth to smudgy image, ill-formed phrase, and slovenly sentence. A mind thus enriched and thus disciplined can know neither slavery nor corruption. The way I commend to you is the way of human emancipation.

PERSONALITY AND WAR

Wickham Steed

ONE day last summer I accepted—rashly, as I have since realised—an invitation from an American publisher to write a book entitled "War and The Common Man". Yet I console myself with the thought that in the writing of books there is one advantage which unfortunate readers of them may not fully understand. This advantage is that—unless he goes on the principle which Schopenhauer denounced so vigorously, and writes his books out of other peoples' books—an author is usually compelled to clear his own mind either before, during, or after the process of writing. In some people clearness of mind is inborn. In others it is the result of long wrestling with facts and ideas until notions are evolved that can stand the test of their parent's own criticism and seem to him fit to be thrown out as a challenge to others. I do not know whether my own mind is endowed with more or less than average clearness; but I do know that when I try to pursue an idea to its ultimate conclusions, or to trace it back to its ascertainable starting-point, so many contingent circumstances and reflections 'butt in' and conspire to blur its outlines as to surround it with a penumbra instead of the hoped-for clarity.

Thus it has been in my thinking about war, both as a collective enterprise and in its bearing upon the human personality. I have found it very hard to be clear. But I make bold to quote the final passage from the first chapter of my still unwritten book:

"Should the nations one day resolve to ban war effectually, it will not be solely because of the risks to life which it entails. War will be banned when its drawbacks are thought greater than its possible benefits or, in other words, because the war-method will be counted over-costly, haphazard, and inadequate. Risk for risk, the risks of what General Smuts has termed 'creative peace' will then be accepted as better worth while than the risks of war, even though the risks of peace involve the sacrifice of many an individual and national sovereignty which men have long held to be more precious than their material possessions or their lives.

Meanwhile, there remains in the concept of war enough of the old glamour, a sufficiency of appeal to patriotism and self-sacrifice, nay, to the ecstasy that men feel when their blood is up or their deeper emotions are stirred, to render its sway over virile minds hard to break. To work against war is really to seek new outlets not merely for the fighting or competitive spirit, but for many a nobler impulse; and to me it seems that the whole issue resolves itself into a question—not lightly to be answered in the affirmative—whether these new outlets can be found and opened to common men in such fashion as to offer them fuller lives, and emotions deeper and more intense even than those which they have hitherto sought in war."

If war is 'the enemy' we ought neither to fall into the error of under-estimating his strength, nor to forget the Latin tag that it is well to learn from him. War appeals to some of the most powerful human instincts—the love of risk or adventure, the spirit of self-devotion, and not less to the lust of power, including power over the lives of other men. However much warlike individuals or nations may have sought to load the dice in their own favour before throwing them in the great gamble of war, they have usually been attracted by the adventurous side of it. Love of adventure, individual and collective, is so fundamental in healthy human beings that it is doubtful whether the idea of non-war will ever gain enough hold over them unless a strong element of chance or risk or 'glorious uncertainty' can be brought into it. Similarly, account must be taken of the lust of power which, as a human motive, is far more potent than pacifists are apt to imagine. A passage from a recent work by a German-Jewish writer, Herr Leopold Schwarzschild, which I have quoted elsewhere, puts this point well. Speaking of the present German desire to build up a formidable military power, and criticising Karl Marx's materialist interpretation of history which most German Socialists accept, Herr Schwarzschild writes:

"It is true that this idea (the potency of the lust of power) contradicts the materialist theory, for the materialist theory knows only one source of history, the economic. But never was it clearer than it is to-day that other things bear upon the lives of peoples and weigh in the balance at least as heavily and automatically as things economic. Questions of power may be such things, for the will to power is not less a material fact than the will to profit, and yearning for power is not always a subsidiary phenomenon of the yearning for gain. It can appear as an end in itself; and the German will to power to-day is, in high degree, of this quality."

I know from experience how true this statement is, not merely of nations with strong military traditions, but likewise of non-military individuals with marked personalities. I have seen the lust of power among great financiers—a craving for the power that wealth gives even more than for wealth itself; and I have noticed it often among successful newspaper proprietors. Indeed, while still a youth, I severed my connection with one of them because my ideas of newspaper power and its proper use differed from his. I thought, foolishly and heretically as it seemed to him, that the right way to gain newspaper power was to disseminate wholesome truths and to sway men by appeals to their minds and hearts rather than to their love of sensation and to emotions of the baser sort. He held that the proper way was to build up a big circulation by sensationalism and then, at a given moment, to tell his millions of readers so to vote in elections as might seem best at the moment. We both wanted power—and I have still a timid preference for my own view of how it should be gained and used. Yet experience has taught me that my method may not yield the swiftest results and that there is something in the American saying: "Everything comes to him who waits, but the hustler gets there first."

Lust of power is not necessarily a mean impulse. It is rarely felt, in dynamic degree, by small or commonplace men. Still, there seems to be an unwritten law that those who gratify it by inferior or reprehensible methods shall be debarred, for reasons inherent in the very inferiority or obliquity of those methods, from using it to the best advantage for themselves and others when once they have gained it. Here the old controversy about the end and the means, whether evil may be done so that good may come, raises its head again and, with it the abstruse mathematical, not to say metaphysical, question whether the quality of any result is not necessarily affected by the methods used to secure it. For instance, it is often said that in political life we need successful business men to manage our national affairs sensibly and well. But how often have not business men, the greater part of whose lives has been spent in looking after their own interests and in making a fortune, turned out to be lamentable failures in the larger arena of national affairs? The broad fact is that intelligent care for the public weal cannot be improvised and that the skilful exercise of it needs special gifts and training, quite as much as any other form of skilful activity. Sometimes I wonder whether the secret of our, on the whole, successful management of our national and imperial affairs, under free institutions and by the method of liberty, may not have lain in our practice of taking men young from families with traditions of public service, and sending them into Parliament and into our departments of State, so that they may acquire public skill and that their outlook may be fashioned from the beginning by higher than personal considerations.

This digression does not wander so far away from our central theme as it may appear at first sight to do. If we reflect upon war as a vehicle for the expression of personality, a field of adventure and an outlet for the lust of power, we find that, as a rule, it has been most successfully utilised by young men of military skill. Alexander the Great, Hannibal, Julius Caesar, Charles XII of Sweden, and Napoleon were all young men who found in war outlets for their genius and satisfaction for their lust of power. During the Great War I remember wondering whether Napoleon, for example, would have been perplexed by the technique of modern warfare and whether it would have prevented him from rising above the undistinguished level of most, if not all, the Allied and enemy commanders; and when I had a chance of putting this question bluntly to Marshal Foch who, of all French soldiers, knew most about Napoleonic strategy and tactics, I seized it eagerly.

The opportunity came early in 1921, when the centenary of Napoleon's death was approaching, and I asked Marshal Foch for a considered estimate of Napoleon's personality and achievements in the light of modern military conditions. He answered:

"In the dark hours of the war we often asked ourselves: 'If Napoleon were to rise from his tomb at the Invalides, what would he say to us, what would he do with our armies of to-day?'

He would have said: 'You have millions of men; I never had them. You have railways, telegraphs, wireless, aircraft, long-range artillery, poison gases; I had none of them. And you do not turn them to account? I'll show you a thing or two!'

He would have taken about six weeks to study and master all these things. Then he would have changed everything from top to bottom, reorganised everything, employed everything in some new way, and would have knocked the bewildered enemy head over heels.

Presently he would have come back at the head of his victorious armies—and would have been a terrible nuisance."

Marshal Foch added that the triumphs of Napoleon are not the most enlightening. They have been thoroughly studied.

His failures, and the reasons for them, are less known, though his unsuccessful campaigns of 1812, 1813, and 1814 are the most interesting of all. And Marshal Foch concluded:

"He failed, they say, because Berthier was no longer with him. I do not think so. In 1814, it is explained, he was already a sick man. Perhaps.

In my view the deep reason for the disaster that overwhelmed him must be sought elsewhere. He forgot that a man cannot be God; that, above the individual, there is the nation; that, above man, there is the moral law; and that war is not the highest goal since, above war, there is Peace."

This is a weighty judgment, for Foch was no mean soldier. I wrote it, in French, after several conversations with him, submitted my text to him for correction or amplification, got it back with one or two slight emendations, and published it, as an article by him, in the Napoleon Centenary Number of *The Times Literary Supplement* in May 1921. I still possess my original manuscript, with his notes upon it, and a letter in which he assured me that I had given perfect expression to his thought.

Thus we return to our question: "If, above war, there is peace", how can the superiority of peace—conceived positively as a state of creative helpfulness, not negatively as non-war—be shown and upheld? How can peace appeal to the young, what adventures can it offer them, what worthy risks can it invite them to take, what opportunities of self-expression and self-fulfilment can it open before them?

There are, of course, the risks of maintaining, as a transitional phase, a state of non-war, that is to say, of ensuring the supremacy of lawful might over lawless force. To this end there must be readiness for police work and willingness to subordinate national sovereignty to some supra-national authority administering an overriding international law. These risks, this curtailment of national freedom, may be hard to face. They will have to be faced, and the young must be educated to face them if war, as an instrument of selfish national policies, is to be a thing of the past.

Doubtless the risks of international police service will appeal to young men of adventurous mind; and the need for such service is, I think, a sufficient warrant for the Officers' Training Corps in our public schools. Fitness to discharge a police function under international law will not need training less perfect, or a less exalted spirit, than fitness to fight for King and country. Nay, if King and country be pledged to stand for non-war, the two ideals may be merged.

But we shall not get far in our work against war without facing, and finding an answer to, the riddle: What is the meaning of life? Founders of religions, sages, and philosophers have sought the answer from time immemorial; yet each generation needs to seek and to find it anew for itself. On New Year's Day, 1935, *The Times* published a letter from Dr Vernon Bartlet of Oxford which touched upon this problem. Referring to the prognostications of doom which the Rev. J. Brown wrote soon after the middle of the eighteenth century, and asking why they were not fulfilled, Dr Bartlet wrote:

"What actually averted further degeneration was the new sense of the sanctity of the human personality—'the soul', as it was then called—latent in every individual, whether rich or poor, cultured or otherwise." Dr Bartlet claimed that this new sense of the sanctity of the human personality grew up in the latter half of the eighteenth century, at least in the English-speaking world, mainly as the result of religious revival. And in the first half of the nineteenth century it gained in reflective clearness from the partial diffusion of Kant's philosophic doctrine—which was itself an interpretation of the Christian doctrine—of the human person, or moral ego, as an end-in-itself, in virtue of its capacity to respond to the inner glow of a duty to strive towards nobler spiritual ideals. This sense has suffered diminution under the shock of the Great War and its secondary psychological and moral effects; and Dr Bartlet averred that "nearly everything in the way of stable and lasting recovery in the material as well as moral health of nations today, including our own, depends on how far and how soon we are able to replace the lost conception of the incomparable value of the human personality in a world where lower but urgent values also have their place and functions".

In a few lines Dr Bartlet thus states the case against all the systems of unfreedom, that is to say, of subordination of the human personality to the authority of a totalitarian State or dictatorship which now prevail in Russia, Italy, and Germany. Into the philosophical aspects of this subordination I have made some enquiry in a little book called *The Meaning of Hitlerism* that was recently published. And had I, at the moment of delivering the lectures upon which this book is based, known of the passage in the Rev. J. Brown's gloomy prophecies which was quoted in *The Times* of December 28, 1934, I should have agreed with that 'gloomy parson' in putting 'the Spirit of Liberty' among 'our remaining virtues' and should have joined in his praise of our 'pure administration of justice'.

Yet to-day our 'spirit of liberty' needs something more than literary recognition. It needs active exercise and open-eyed support even to the extent of taking some risks on its behalf. In it we hold a treasure for which the world is waiting, a treasure more precious than tons of hoarded gold. Without the spirit of liberty there can be no true development of the human personality—provided always that the spirit of individual freedom be accompanied by an equal sense of individual responsibility, by individual self-government implying self-discipline, and that the doctrines of unfreedom be met and overcome by the power of conviction in individual minds, or wills, or souls, working itself out in individual character and conduct.

One of the strongest counts against war is that it engenders a spirit of violence which, even when international warfare has ceased, is apt to work itself out in a kind of gangsterdom that suppresses individual thought and freedom of speech and seeks to replace them by a State-organised 'collective mind'. It exalts this artificial 'mass-mind' above individual minds, and preaches extreme racialism and international violence, that is to say, war, against other nations as the method of attaining race-supremacy. As long as this tendency prevails among powerful peoples, mankind will be far from non-war, to say nothing of peace.

We have so long thought of war as the antithesis of peace that we find it hard to rid our minds of the fallacious notion that non-war and peace are synonymous. We turn our scientific discoveries to war purposes, and scarcely pause to reflect what scientific works of peace might be in a warless world. A recent exploit may help to stir our imaginations. The casting of the 200-inch reflector at Corning in the United States for the great telescope that is to be set up on Mount Wilson in California is an event truly notable. One need not be an astronomer to understand its importance, nor a maker of glass to share the thrill of the men who prepared the scores of tons of molten silica and other ingredients that went to the pouring of that incandescent compound into the great mould where it will take ten months to cool. Then will come the months of careful polishing, the transport of the finished product across the American Continent, and its fixing in the giant instrument that is designed to widen and to deepen our understanding of the universe.

This is eminently a work of peace. It is being done by private initiative, guided by schooled and expert imagination and sustained by a spirit of high adventure. Were it possible to employ in other scientific adventures, great and small, a tithe of the funds and of the spirit of invention now expended upon preparation for war, what progress might not be made in wresting from nature more of her baffling secrets and in giving new meaning to human life ! Those who have seen the scientific exhibition at South Kensington will understand how diversified are the fields that still remain to be explored, what scope for human personality the exploration might offer, and how small and timid, in comparison with what might be, are the steps yet taken to gratify the sanest and the best of all forms of the lust of power—power both over the material world in which we live, and power to know and to utilise the myriad truths that are still hidden from us in regions less material.

Indeed, it may fairly be asked whether to-day there is a clear line of demarcation between the material and the spiritual. The daily miracle of wireless communication is an ever-present reminder of the reality of the things unseen—just as preparations for 'scientific' warfare and the harnessing of technical and chemical knowledge to the work of destruction are reminders that our moral progress limps sadly and tardily behind even our present knowledge. Centuries ago, Leonardo da Vinci—an outstanding genius whose achievements have not always been appreciated at their true worth—discovered the principles of the submarine and the aeroplane. His aeroplane might not have worked without the internal combustion engine; but so fearful was he lest his submarine be put to devilish purposes in war that he turned away from his discovery and hid it. He had no faith that the morality of his times would be proof against the temptation to turn it into an engine of damnation.

Our age has been less squeamish. It has not hesitated to use the results of scientific research and invention in ways that must mean, unless they be renounced or otherwise prohibited, the end of modern civilisation itself. The really revolting side of war is not so much its destructiveness as its stupidity—the stupidity of killing, maiming, and annihilating instead of the intelligence of creating, helping, and building up. There are innumerable outlets for personalities, including the strongest and the most masterful, in this immense task of turning the minds of men away from the adventure of spoiling their human inheritance and towards the greater adventure of developing it, drawing from it all that it can give to our present limited capacities and preparing a wider scope for the higher capacities that may be evolved in proportion as opportunity for their employment opens up.

We need, verily, a new philosophy of life which, after all, need not be so very new because it might be drawn from the Aristotelian principle that the source of true gladness lies in activity that approaches the fulfilment of its purpose, the quality of the gladness being conditioned by the nobility of aim which the activity serves. Sometimes I think I can see what men might do in a world beyond war and the fear of war, a world in which a cry of distress from any quarter of the globe would be an instant summons to human helpfulness everywhere, a world in which famine and pestilence would challenge collective endeavour to overcome them by un-rewarded national effort and personal self-sacrifice. In such a world frontiers would be as invisible as the borders of English counties, and nations would seek glory above that of other nations in willingness and ability to serve mankind most greatly. The spirit of emulation need not disappear or, indeed, the spirit of adventure. What should and must disappear or be suppressed is the spirit of envy, greed, and lust of power for power's sake. We shall overcome war when we begin to fit ourselves for the great adventure of peace, an adventure thrilling enough since it must imply a radical transformation of social structures, a transmutation of political and economic 'values', a change in the standards of honour—personal, national and international—a complete revolution, in short, save in the sense that men need never change the highest con-ception of human worth, that of supreme ability unselfishly to serve their fellow men. The chief outlet for personality in a world beyond war will be found in its dedication to human service, in fitness to serve, and in readiness to face whatever risks such service may entail.

THE MODERN MOVEMENT
IN EDUCATION

Laurin Zilliacus

To me "the modern movement in education" means that body of theory and practice which is generally known as the New Education. There is a peculiar difficulty in speaking about this movement in England, and in particular to a Public School audience. The difficulty is this: a survey of the New Education must include a great deal that is common practice and common outlook throughout English education of to-day and some that has long been so, particularly in the Public Schools. A Continental observer coming fresh to the English educational world would bracket the long-established educational institution that is giving our Conference hospitality with the more radical of the newer educational ventures under the common heading "New Schools". He would see less difference between them than between either of them and the old type of school in his own country. The boundary line between old and new is not easy to trace in England. That is of course wholly a thing to rejoice at, but it renders difficult the task of the lecturer on New Education.

"New" is in any case an unsatisfactory term, and certainly not one to be taken literally. No educational movement of any value can be new in more than a very limited use of the word, new in certain details or new in a shifting of emphasis, a re-grouping of old factors. (You will note that I am cautious in my introductory words—there is Scotch blood in me though I am not aware of any other non-Aryan admixture.)

I have been allowed to divide what I have to put before you into two talks, and I propose in the first of these to try and sketch an outline of this (partly) New Education as it appeared before the War, and then of its development along certain lines as a consequence of that ghastly event. In my second talk I shall try and deal with the challenge that in our own times has been levelled at the "New" as well as at all other conceptions of education.

To begin with, I shall ask you to assist at the birth or rather births of what was significantly called the New School Movement before it was termed the New Education.

The first New Schools were established in England in the eighties and nineties—by Public School men. Reddie of Abbotsholme and Badley of Bedales are the pioneer names. Badley himself describes what he was doing as "a modification of our Public School system, an attempt to keep what is best in that great tradition while enlarging its scope".

A number of years later the first experimental schools of similar type were founded in America. As far as I have been able to find out, they arose independently of the English experiments, indeed (by a little humorous twist of fate) they were evolved in that country of the "practical" man as the result of the armchair speculations of a university professor. In Asia, still later, but also apparently independently, other New Schools were established. On the Continent of Europe, on the other hand, the New School Movement seems to have been directly inspired by example from England. In France, indeed, the first step was the publication of a book entitled *A quoi tient la supériorité des Anglo-Saxons?* (The author was not referring to that sense of superiority occasionally displayed by English tourists, but to a superiority the author himself felt in the Anglo-Saxon.) The reply given by the author was: English education, and in particular English boarding school education. It is notable that though he was attracted by certain specific New Schools, he considered them and the Public School system in general to display the same essential characteristics. In Germany, theory soon ran riot, with chapters devoted to definitions of terms and whole books published to refute or modify the definitions of the other fellow. But the first practical consequences there, too, were boarding schools, which were called Landerziehungsheime (Country Educational Homes) and were founded to give German youth the benefits of the English boarding school. The immediate source of inspiration was once more the New Boarding School, but no sharp distinction was drawn between it and its older brethren.

Thus was born the New School Movement. I suppose it became a "movement" when the pioneer schools grew numerous enough to attract the attention of each other and the general public.

I will now ask you to come with me on a rapid tour of the typical New Schools at the time of the outbreak of the War, noting certain outstanding features. Some of these we shall find more in evidence in some schools, some in others. Some you will recognise as long traditional in your own schools, others recently introduced there. When you do, please take this as a reason for basking in "la supériorité des Anglo-Saxons" rather than as a reason for quarrelling with the term New School.

The first characteristic I think we shall notice is the *many-sidedness*, the richness of the life as compared with that in the old school in most countries. The typical continental school is still in our times an institution for imparting knowledge when it is not simply an institution for cramming for examinations. This is apparent already in the names given on the Continent to that branch of Government which is concerned with schools, e.g. Ministère de l'Instruction Publique, Unterrichtsministerium, Undervisningsministeriet. Contrast 'Board of Education' in England. English education has long conceived its aim widely. The Public School has at least aimed at developing the gentleman and has realised that he is a creature with a body, with emotions and will (character) as well as intellect. That is why you have long had your games with all that these call for and develop of physical fitness, endurance, "going all out" and yet retaining control, team work and team spirit, a sense of fair play, and ability to treat the " two imposters triumph and disaster" just the same. That, too, is why you have had your prefect system and your house system with all that these imply of training in public service and self-discipline and of sensitiveness to unwritten as well as written rules of conduct, of leadership as well as of obedience to authority.

Having proffered these bouquets, I feel I may risk passing on to you certain criticisms as well, criticisms levelled both by outsiders and by the Public School men who founded their New Schools: that too much was made of games, which are after all only games; that the school was too narrow and closed a little community and the public spirit engendered too limited in scope and too foreign to the needs of the world outside. Be this as it may, no one can deny that the concept of education as something more than imparting knowledge has long and respectable standing in the Public School. On the Continent this concept was both new and a fundamental characteristic of the pioneer schools in the eighties.

In these, therefore, we find numerous forms of self-government, and we find much made of the development of the body (games are generally supplemented by physical training under competent guidance, by gardening or care of the school estate, and by other forms of outdoor exercise having close relation to the life of labour in the adult world). We find what is now a commonplace, but was not so at the time of the first New Schools; a wide choice of studies, with the possibility of taking science or modern languages as central subjects and not only classics, and we find the arts given an honourable place in the curriculum. Indeed, in the typical New School, the study of art and to some extent the practice of various forms of art (including of course music and literature) is woven into the work in many "subjects" outside the arts and crafts themselves. The programme of these schools is shot through with the products of personal creative work, often of considerable artistic merit. We find it in individual notebooks, in the joint product of a group of children, such as, for instance, a book, a chart, a map, a dramatisation or a joint account of some phase of the work laid before another form or group of forms at a school "assembly". But I must not spend too long on this first characteristic of New Schools. I will merely add that the many-sided school life includes a number of vigorous societies (dramatic, literary, scientific, engineering, sociological, etc.), a feature which is familiar enough in any good English school.

If we step from an old to a New School, a second characteristic which is also far more obvious abroad than in England is the *activity* prevalent. I am here not thinking merely of the fact that head and hand are both enlisted in laboratories and workshops, but of the active method of study in all subjects. New knowledge is not simply learnt from a text-book; something is *done* with it: e.g. it is extracted from different sources and summarised in a written account or map or diagram or graph, or it is used as material for a lecture or creative work, or it is incorporated in the findings of a group of research workers and there made the subject of discussion and criticism before it is accepted.

We shall often find classrooms in New Schools equipped with light tables and chairs instead of desks, and see these arranged in different ways at different times. Some children will be sitting alone, others will have joined together into smaller or larger groups. There will be coming and going between libraries, art room, laboratories, workshops, and the classroom. This supplies the necessary physical conditions for "learning by doing", the aim of which is not merely to charge knowledge with meaning, but also to develop initiative and practical ability.

Among the names given to the New School and disputed in the works of the theorists is that of the *Free School*. Freedom is undoubtedly one of the noticeable features that will strike us on our rapid tour: freedom of choice among studies and occupations, so that everyone has an opportunity of finding employment where he can best make his mark, freedom in planning one's work and in methods of work (the Dalton Plan may be cited as one of the numerous ways of ensuring this freedom), freedom in the informal relationships between young and old, in the small number of rules and restrictions and the small amount of surveillance (this implies freedom to make mistakes and learn by them and to evolve genuine tastes and standards), in the large spaces of wholly free time. (This is all the more necessary in New Schools, where the richness and variety of life easily lead to an overcrowded time-table. One must of course have leisure in order to learn to use it.) We shall notice, too, a wide measure of freedom for the teacher—freedom, that is, for each one to build up his own course and work out his own methods.

Closely allied to the large measure of freedom accorded both young and old is *the respect for individuality* that characterises the New Schools. Realisation of the value of personality and appreciation of its uniqueness is well in the English tradition, and I know no country where adult society is equally tolerant. The young of species *homo sapiens* is, however, notoriously intolerant, and in its hands "good form" (which may clothe itself in incredible trivialities) has been known to give personal idiosyncrasies a rough passage. I think, however, that we shall find on our tour of inspection a considerable measure of tolerance even among the young in the New Schools. In this one respect I think we shall find a New School feature more prominent on the Continent than in England. The great god Good Form has for better or for worse less undisputed sway abroad than among the youth of England (I feel that this is connected with another curious fact, that it is more difficult to raise a blush on the cheek of a Continental than on that of an Englishman).—Consideration for individuality does not, however, only show itself in tolerance. It also takes the form of special care for each individual, i.e. on the one hand diagnosis of his weak points, and the giving of special help to overcome these, and on the other hand provision for the exercise of individual talents and interests.

A fifth characteristic we shall notice in relatively few schools at the time of the War, though it has since become more and more prominent. This is *the breaking down of boundaries between related subjects*. In the primary stage of education this is more easily accomplished than in the secondary. In the primary stage it is not so difficult to find one teacher capable of teaching several of the accepted school subjects and therefore also able to set work that cuts across them and shows their inter-relationship. In the secondary stage your master of one trade is less likely to be Jack of several, except of the closest relatives: science and mathematics, history and literature, biology and geography, are examples that spring to the mind. For the rest we shall find a synthesis between subjects achieved only where different members of the staff are willing to co-operate intimately—a somewhat rare phenomenon but one which has shown itself to be essential for the development of the New School.

The sixth and last characteristic that I particularly want to underline is not so easily seen on a hasty inspection, but becomes evident on closer study of any good New School. It may be described as *the co-operation of the pupil in his own education*, or in other words, enlisting the will of the victim of our benevolent efforts in favour of those efforts. I do not mean sitting down with a boy and saying "Now, what do you think would be advisable for your education", or persuading him to draw up a list of desirable qualities, and assign marks to himself in these daily, like Benjamin Franklin.

I have seen examples of something very much like this, and I admit the danger of developing prigs and egocentrics in a form of education that places the individual child in the centre of the stage. (I shall have more to say on this point in my second lecture.) I am not, however, here concerned with aberrations of modern education any more than with drawing a boundary between it and "old" education, but rather with pointing out factors that are of positive interest. Among these I should certainly list an atmosphere of good-will, of interest in work for its own sake rather than for the sake of gaining marks, of teacher-pursuing (by children seeking help with what they feel to be their work) rather than of pupil-pursuing (by imposers of work which the evaders feel to be no concern of theirs). This atmosphere is a precious thing. It explains most of what is of value in education. It changes the classroom from a battlefield to a laboratory, a studio, a place of co-operation profitable to all parties, and even at times to a hallowed spot where disciples are gathered together about a master, and it renders association between young and old pleasurable and natural outside the classroom as well as during working hours. It flows, as all good things in the long run do, from the Head Master and the members of the Staff, and it depends on their fundamental attitude towards education. I shall have more to say on this point presently. For the moment I am satisfied to point out that this fundamental attitude is essential, and wish immediately to add that it is also essential for the attitude to find expression in carefully worked out teaching method.

I have seen many ways used to bring to the boy a genuine sense of purpose in his work. One which is negative but common to most New Schools is the drastic diminution of extraneous rewards and punishments and the abolition of competitive marking. Orders of merit where one man's meat is another man's poison seem to most modern educators not only to introduce an extraneous and second-rate motive for the pursuit of knowledge and to put the teacher in the position of arbiter of fates rather than of being a source of help and guidance, but they seem to do something worse: to accustom the growing generation to a deplorable feature in competitive society.

The whole question of numerical marking is complex, and

forms part of the larger question of examining and rating. I cannot go into it here, but may point out that there are parts of the school course that can be evaluated with figures, such as, for example, speed and skill in arithmetical operations, knowledge of specific facts in mathematics, grammar, vocabulary, spelling, or generally accepted relationships between groups of facts in history, geography, science. In such matters exact assessment is not only possible, it can be done by the boy himself with the aid of well-made, standardised tests. In good New School practice we shall find such testing done and powerfully contributing to making the tester (who is also the tested) feel that progress in his studies is his own concern. (Incidentally it does much to lay the spectre of cheating in school. I believe that this spectre is not very formidable when confronted by "la supériorité des Anglo-Saxons", but in schools of the older type abroad it is a serious matter. Cheating at tests administered by yourself is like cheating at patience. There are individuals who do it, but the satisfaction must be small.)

In those parts of the school work that cannot be evaluated numerically—i.e. by far the most important parts—we shall find certain New Schools boldly acknowledging the facts and seeking other ways to stimulate good work and to judge the result. Learning by doing often results in tangible products, and there are of course ways of submitting these to the criticism of the boy himself, his fellows or his teachers, ways that tend to bring about an attitude of concern for the quality and quantity of the work rather than concern for sliding out of it or garnering marks. Contributing to group work naturally tends the same way. Another method employed is to link the work in various subjects to problems or undertakings important in the life of the school. Where a piece of work is needed for the school magazine, for a lecture or a play, for the school bank or stationery shop, there is no difficulty in making its purpose both obvious and appealing.

Through these and other ways that those who wish to study the New Schools will find for themselves, the desired attitude is built up, a capital is accumulated on which to fall back on the frequent occasions when the work is dull and the purpose not evident to any but the teacher (sometimes, perhaps, not even to him but only to the examiner, or behind him to the god of pedantry). This capital is largely composed of faith, faith in the authority and good-will of the teacher, and its strength will depend on the teacher's own fundamental attitude towards education and the amount of effort he has put into evolving expression for this attitude in methods of work.

*   *   *   *   *

We have finished our rapid tour of inspection. If I have in any measure succeeded in making you see the essential features through my eyes, you will have noted the following six: many-sidedness of the curriculum, activity, freedom, individual treatment, fusion of related subjects, and co-operation between teacher and taught.

I have deliberately pointed out characteristics—outwardly visible signs of the New Education rather than high points of its theory—because I think that this corresponds to the way in which the New Education has come about. As someone has remarked, educational pioneers have generally been better at running schools than at describing them. I should even go so far as to say that the development of modern educational theory has consisted, and still largely consists, of analysing the principles implied in the intuitively created practice of pioneer schoolmasters. I have, however, tried to sketch the characteristic features of the New Schools in such a way that the principles immediately underlying them readily emerge. It is obvious, for instance, that the presence of a large measure of freedom in a school implies a belief in the principle of freedom on the part of the educator, and similar deductions may be made from the other characteristics described.

There are, however, two principles that seem to me to underlie all the others and so to be worth special attention. One of these I should call the *principle of development*, the other the *principle of wholeness*.

Education is development—an aiding of the growth—of something already present in a latent or undeveloped state rather than a process of moulding or a process of addition. To make this clear by way of contrast: the "exam. and cram" or Knowledge School acts on the principle that education is a process of adding something from the outside (i.e. adding a given set of technical abilities and a fixed body of knowledge). The schools in the countries under dictatorships, on the other hand, seem to be actuated by the principle that education is a process of moulding. The pattern is given, and the growing generation is moulded in accordance with it.

It is difficult to explain what I see as the principle of development without seeming either to advocate "laisser faire" or to be presenting you with mere wind. Aristotle has somewhere said (those of you who have read the classics will no doubt recall the exact words) that objects in nature are such as, actuated by a force of their own, move towards a developed state inherent in themselves. The New Education regards Man as an object in nature, and can no more be satisfied with "laisser faire" than a gardener can when he wants a tulip bulb to develop into a flowering tulip. He must arrange its surroundings and give it the kind of care called for by its needs. A man is more complex than a tulip bulb, his needs more manifold and difficult to ascertain, and the developed state towards which he is moving more varied as between individuals of the species and less easy to know in advance. The educator will therefore make more mistakes than the gardener. He will have to take more risks and operate more with guesses, but his function is fundamentally the same. He has to arrange the educational surroundings—the school— as "naturally" as possible, i.e. as true to life in our world as possible, so that the values that operate in human society will make themselves felt, the lessons of real life be learned and the different sides that human nature has shown itself to have will all have an opportunity to develop. I think you will find that each of the characteristics we have seen in New School practice has a contribution to make towards carrying out this principle. I think, too, you will see that it calls for a "hands off" policy, a policy of observation and sympathy and patience rather than of brusque or frequent interference.

In the sphere of knowledge the principle of development also has application. It may there be described as the Here and Now principle: start with the body of facts and experience already possessed by those you desire to teach; start, that is, with what makes up the daily lives of the pupils and their parents (their food, shelter, lighting, clothing, transport, work and play, social institutions, etc.); study that, arrive at generalisations through the familiar and particular, associate these in time and place till you have a background of historical, scientific, and geographical knowledge. Aim, that is, at making the growing child more at home in its world, at giving it a better understanding of the life it is leading rather than at giving it the contents of certain fixed courses in certain artificially isolated subjects.

The Here and Now principle leads to a revolutionary change in the school curriculum if taken seriously. This has been done in certain rural schools with most interesting results, while some application of the principle is common in most New Schools. Indeed, if we leap for a moment from the educational world of 1914 which we are surveying to that of to-day, we shall find that the curricula of most New Schools are made up in varying proportions of one part arrived at by following the Here and Now principle (e.g. studies of current events, local surveys, activities and studies connected with institutions of practical importance in the school or the community outside), and of another part arrived at by following the addition principle (i.e. fixed courses built up by working backwards from a given end point).

The other principle that I believe to underlie New Education practice—the principle of *wholeness*—is psychological. It states that Man is a being striving after integration and harmony, in a word, after wholeness. The educator should always keep this human tendency in view. It follows in the first place that education should concern itself with the all-round development of the child and not with only certain sides of his nature. In the second place, it means that we should realise that we are at any and every moment affecting the whole child, that no part of its person can function in isolation. This means that we cannot deal with the emotions and leave the intellect unaffected, or *vice versâ*, and that we should not try and present mutually contradictory ideas even if we separate them in time. We cannot, for example, if we wish to aid in growth towards wholeness, teach through the intellect that Christianity is a religion of love while the child is actually experiencing it as fear or even as boredom. We cannot teach that science is experimental and inductive by methods that are authoritative and deductive. We cannot devote two periods a week to developing a sense of beauty, and sin against, or encourage the child to sin against, this sense in the work done during the other periods. We cannot go on adding new subjects to the time-table for each new area of knowledge that comes to seem desirable or squeeze in new courses of exercises for each new quality that seems desirable in the growing generation. There is a marked tendency to do this in our times. I have seen specific courses given (or the school urged to give them) in sobriety, in reverence for and the right use of the national flag, in crossing streets safely, in love of country. Such aberrations are products of the atomistic, the brick-building view of human nature.

The wholeness principle tells us that each addition we wish to make to our curriculum must be joined organically —fused—with what we already have there, and that in what we already have there we must achieve harmony and mutual support. That is why we have found on our tour of inspection.

that the New Schools were breaking down boundaries between subjects. That, too, is why we find a single piece of work (say a jointly made chart of a certain historical period or a dramatic production or a large map) so planned that those doing it are at one and the same time exercised in discussion and co-operation, in directing and in accepting direction, in the use of books and other source material, in orderliness and a sense of beauty, all the while their memories are being stored with knowledge.

*   *   *   *   *   *

What I have hitherto said has not, I hope, made education appear to be a branch of science or of engineering, in which you formulate certain principles, work out certain technical methods for applying these and then go ahead. That is unfortunately the view prevailing in many Education Departments, though evidently not in that of England, which leaves the individual school the widest possible freedom in curriculum and teaching methods.

Education is an art. The artist may study theories and learn technique, but his art is not created by these: he has to rise above them. He does not always succeed, which is no doubt why art schools are sometimes decried as destroying art and training schools as making education mediocre. Another way of admitting that education is an art is to say that the individual educator is more important than methods and theories. "Take care of the staff and the school will take care of itself" may be a truism, but it certainly is true, as every experienced Head Master knows. We shall not understand the education built up by the pioneers of the modern movement without attempting to understand their persons. I must therefore ask you to take a deep breath and plunge with me into the soul of the New Educator, descending with me below the level of the conscious intellect to that of the emotional attitude underneath.

We shall find there, I believe, *faith in human nature*—faith, that is, both in the nature of the individual and of society as a whole. The New Educator believes in Aristotle's dictum. He is therefore content to arrange "natural" surroundings for his charges and he is confident that they will then move towards that state which is inherent in themselves. He is able to see education as a development, not as a process of adding or moulding.

We shall, too, find that the New Educator approaches life, and in particular his fellow beings, as an artist. His view of them is therefore intuitive rather than scientific and theorising. It is global and not atomistic. He is prepared for surprises, and does not *a priori* think he knows all about the life process. He has the artist's respect for personality.

We shall find the New Educator an idealist. I admit that this is a dangerous term; indeed in our day, almost an improper term like the word "mother" in the *Brave New World*, and yet I cannot get away from it except by using the word 'religious' instead. I know New Educators who are Catholics, Protestants, Jews, Mahommedans, agnostics, and even fierce atheists; but none that are not idealist in the sense of being at bottom moved by a passion for certain permanent values in the human tradition. The New Educator feels he is working for a cause, even when his is an isolated effort without an organisation to back it.

The worker for a cause is in danger of becoming inhuman, which is the last thing an educator should be. The educator has to have his eye on persons, not on a theory, and his heart in tune with each individual. It is safe to say that the great educators have known how to temper their idealism with compassion. They have been sensitive to what Russell has called "the cry that is in every man".

The New Educator, as I see him, is therefore an artist. He has faith in human nature. He has warmth and tenderness. He has dedicated himself to serve in the great adventure of Man through the ages.

*   *   *   *   *   *

I have now given an outline picture, as I see it, of the pioneers of education who gave us their New Schools in the far-off, apparently changeless, days before the War, of their principles, whether consciously formulated or not, and of the distinguishing marks of their educational practice. I should not have spent practically the whole time at my disposal to-day on this picture if I did not think it contained much of permanent value to all interested in education; indeed, much that was in education before their time and much that has since become commonplace.

The War years saw the idealistic aspect of education forced into the focus of consciousness. Idealism, as someone has recently said, is the offspring of suffering and hope. Education became in the public consciousness a cause—the cause of saving humanity from catastrophe. The years since 1918 have seen an ever-increasing number of educational conferences, a swelling body of advanced educational legislation, and a flood of educational literature.

Two years after the Peace Conference, a meeting was called in Calais of people who believed in building a new world through education. There were Germans present at this meeting, which thus was, I believe, the first international conference to welcome ex-enemies. The moving spirits were Mrs Beatrice Ensor, the present Executive Director of the New Education Fellowship, and with her the well-known writer on educational topics, Dr A. Ferrière, and Dr Elizabeth Rotten, who is held in grateful remembrance by many a prisoner in Ruhleben and other German internment camps. The primary interest of these leaders was in peace, social justice, and a rebirth of mankind, and they looked on schools as one means of working towards their goal. An international outlook was a fundamental part of their purpose. They called themselves the New Education Fellowship. They were, as you see, cranks, i.e. they held views to-day that will be commonly accepted (possibly too late) to-morrow. They agreed to meet in biennial conferences, which were later made triennial. Their organisation grew rapidly, until at the present day it is world-wide, and its membership is expressed by a high four-figure number.

With the rapid growth came a certain change in character. The New Education Fellowship is now, above all, an association of practical educators whom it serves in a large number of wholly practical ways. Its conferences have retained much of the vision and drive that characterised the meeting at Calais, but they now also offer study courses, exhibitions of method and material, and an interchange of experience between people faced by similar problems in schools all over the world. In my opinion the Fellowship has done work of importance in breaking down the isolation of educational experimenters and in bringing home to teachers the international nature of the world in which we live.

*   *   *   *   *   *

I began this talk by inviting you to join in a rapid tour of the schools which, started in the eighties by Public School men, grew into the modern movement in education. I pointed out what seemed to me to be characteristics which distinguished these schools from their contemporaries and which may be indicated by the following labels: a many-sided curriculum including a large amount of creative activity, learning by doing, freedom and tolerance, consideration for individuality, and enlisting the will of the child in his own education. I then attempted to analyse the principles implicit in these characteristics and described them as the principle of development and the principle of wholeness. After this I tried to trace these principles to their sources in the nature of the educator, whom I considered to be a person who has faith in human nature, who approaches his profession and his fellows as an artist although he is willing to use science in applying his art, and who is an idealist in the sense of being actuated primarily by a desire to identify himself with the adventure of mankind. Finally, I tried to show how the tragic experiences of the War brought to a focus the "serving a cause" nature of education and how, through the institution of an international organisation, it became apparent that the educational problem and its progressive solution transcends national boundaries. I think we can summarise the whole modern movement in education by saying that it has conceived its purpose to be what I understand has been chosen as the central theme of this conference, "the development of personality in an international world".

To-morrow, when I shall again have the pleasure of addressing you, I shall seek to show how recent events have challenged this, as well as every current conception of the function of the school in society.

EDUCATION FOR WORLD
CITIZENSHIP

Laurin Zilliacus

I ASK you this morning to come with me first into a school
under the Hitler régime. We shall look into the lecture hall—
a large modern room packed with a profoundly interested
audience consisting of parents and children and members of
the teaching staff. The lecturer, from the capital of the Reich,
is elucidating recent history, bringing it up to date, and
putting it, of course, in a way that meets the approval of the
powers that be. The audience approves too. They hang on
every phrase and when the "Heil Hitler" cries drown a word
the lecturer pauses to repeat it. Presently, the account reaches
the fateful night of June 30th last year when, as you know,
a number of trusted and high officials of the realm, and
with them numerous less important persons, were seized and
shot.

The lecturer at this point leans over the rostrum and asks
a rhetorical question. "You may ask me 'Why did not
Hitler, who knows everything that is going on, de-mask the
traitor von Röhm* at an earlier stage, and cut short his evil
activities?'" A pause, and the lecturer goes on. "Well,
I ask you, why did not Christ at an earlier stage de-mask
the traitor Judas Iscariot and prevent his evil activities?"
The applause is terrific.

What are we to think of this? I turn to my left hand, and
the answer is "blasphemous, repulsive hysteria". I turn to
my right, and the answer is "patriotic fervour", while a cynical
voice in between whispers that these are sometimes difficult
to distinguish. Sober reflection, however, points out that
whatever else may be said, we must admit that we have here

* von Röhm, the Organiser of the S.A. (the Brown Shirt
association), was one of the highest and most trusted officials.

enthusiasm, enthusiasm shown not only one day, but day after day over a long period of time, enthusiasm which is apparent in old and young alike.

We leave the lecturer and wander into the geography room. We find upon one whole wall maps of the world, upon which information is piled as only German ingenuity and thoroughness pile it. What stands out more than anything else is political information. We see the boundaries of Germany before the Treaty of Versailles and the boundaries to-day. The areas which it is the duty of every German to strive to bring into the Fatherland again are shaded. There are diagrammatic pictures of the armed forces of other countries and beside them in comparative size pictures of a tiny German force with an obvious inference to be drawn. There are pictures of the colonies which once belonged to Germany and are now gone.

We go on to the history class and find that they are not dealing with "1066 and All That" but with recent history, the history of the last thirty years—history if you are willing to give it that name, i.e. an exposition of the last thirty years from the point of view of the powers that be. If we go into classes in subjects which by their nature are more neutral, say arithmetic or experimental science, we shall of course not find a great difference between Nazi practice and the usual. But we find the courses in these subjects cut down so as to give more time for the "propaganda" courses, and we find the work even in these neutral subjects definitely conceived as a preparation of the student for taking part in the life of the nation. The boy who is doing, say, experimental science, is made to feel that his skill and knowledge are likely to be wanted in the service of the country. Everything he does is linked on to the claims of one of the many "fronts" into which the whole of life is divided.

If we look at the so-called free time of the children, we find that it, too, is carefully organised. Boys and girls are gathered in various "youth organisations", they are sent out on excursions with a flag at their head, patriotic songs are sung, the beauties of the Fatherland are pointed out, and its ideals preached. There is a great deal of exercising indistinguishable from military drill and significantly called "arms sports" (*Wehrsport*).

If we go to another country under a dictatorship—Italy—we shall find something very similar, though perhaps somewhat less harsh, for the Italians have been going for a longer time, both as members of civilised human society and as subjects of a dictatorship. In the schools we find, however, the same enthusiasm, the same linking of the work with the world outside the school. Here, too, the children are organised into groups for their free time. From the age of eight onwards they go into camp and are trained excellently physically, but in definite military technique and in a military spirit.

If we go to another dictatorship at the opposite pole—Russia—we also find something very similar. We find the same enthusiasm in schools and the same intimate linking of the school with the life outside. Here the link is, in fact, so close that we find a particular school in a kind of symbiosis with a particular factory or a particular collective farm. We shall find, too, I believe, that the free time of the children is organised and that in it they are given a training which is military in type and militaristic in spirit.

Under dictatorships, whether of the right or left, the feature most noticeable is that *school and society have been made into one organic unit.* Youth in the schools feels that it has a mission, that it is taking an important part in the life and work of the community. It is, further, learning to know what life in the adult world is like both by studying it intellectually and by taking a practical part in it. Even if we do not like this system we must admit that it has a sound psychological foundation. It appeals to one of the most fundamental urges of human nature, on the one hand to what the psychologist Adler has described as the desire to be "on the useful side", i.e. the urge to do something significant, the desire to feel you are important, and on the other to its counterpart, the urge to devotion, obedience, sacrifice for a cause.

If we turn to schools under a democratic régime, do we see the same thing? Are school and society one? Does youth feel that it has a mission, that what it is doing is important, is service in a sacred cause? Does the school work help the growing generation to understand the life of our day? I think the answer must be largely negative. Certainly an entire negative so far as "exam. and cram" goes. Youth in the schools in a democratic state neither shares nor studies the life of the adult community.

The "exam. and cram" system works, so far as I understand it, on what we may call the application theory. According to this theory you sharpen the faculties on any convenient subject; and then, once sharpened, they can be vicariously applied. For instance, you sharpen a person's power of thought by an analysis of Latin syntax or by mathematics; and then when he requires clear and independent judgment to solve a social or economic problem, he will take out this tool and use it. Unfortunately, the human mind does not work that way. Training is willy nilly specific; what we can transfer from one field of activity to another is not very much unless the fields of activity are closely related.

I have recently been sent a booklet on Education for Citizenship, issued by the Association for Education in Citizenship, of which I hope Mr Spencer Leeson will tell us more to-morrow. In it Sir Ernest Simon writes: "The point of view frequently found to-day among educationalists is that since the quality of the citizen is determined by his whole character we can best attain the desired end by the *indirect* method of endeavouring to turn out young people sound in body and mind, equipped both with the tools which will enable them to earn a living and with some knowledge of the cultural and ethical inheritance of civilisation." "But", he continues, "irrelevant learning, of however high a type, does not make a complete citizen. A man who is the highest authority on the use of the Greek particle or on the latest theories of physical science is not necessarily capable of forming a sensible opinion about the value of the League of Nations or of the relative merits of Free Trade and Tariff Reform or even of judging wisely the type of man who will make the best Member of Parliament or Minister of the Crown."

And he goes on:

"The political world is so complex and difficult that it is as essential to train men just as consciously and deliberately for their duties as citizens as for vocations or professions."

In the opening address to this conference (in so far as the newspaper report gives the words of the speaker accurately), Lord Eustace Percy described the youth brought up in our schools in the following terms:

"Particularly do they not think in that most important sphere of human activity, the relation of man to man, the relation of man to society, the way society ought to be governed, and particularly on the conduct of nations, man in his relation to the world, man in his relation to God."

I have had much opportunity of seeing the application theory work out and I can assure you that my experience leads me to agree with the findings of theoretical psychology, i.e. that it is not of much value.

What then of the psychological basis of education in democratic countries? Does the school appeal to strong, deep-lying motives? Well, in a narrowly limited sphere, in certain schools—yes. I am referring to that Lilliputian world for which service is really claimed in seriousness and enthusiasm and loyalty are awakened: the world of games and prefectship. Outside this—no. Certainly not in what makes up the greater part of school life: the work in the different courses of study. Here we have nothing like the enthusiasm to show that gives life to the dictatorship school. The reason is obvious: we are appealing to motives that are trivial and second-rate in comparison to the urge of giving body and soul in a great cause. The motives we touch are crudely egoistic: the desire for marks, for avoiding penalties, for being first, for passing an examination—these are our psychological stock in trade. Of course, more satisfying and educationally fruitful motives are touched as well: the urge to create, to satisfy an intellectual interest, to master some new area of knowledge or acquire a new form of skill. But these are for the exceptional teacher, the exceptional child, and the exceptional moment when the routine demands have been satisfied, and they do not in any case make a strong *social* appeal.

Small wonder that our schools appear ephemeral institutions, floating in the academic upper air, in comparison with the firmly anchored Servant of the State in lands under dictatorial rule.

Up to this point it may have sounded as if I admired the dictatorship schools. I certainly do admire their good points; but I feel the bad points strongly too. It seems to me indefensible to use children as pawns in the battles of grown-up people and to force on immature minds a series of ready-made prejudices. It seems to me wrong to try and mould the rising generation after a predetermined pattern. It seems to me abominable to inculcate hatred in children, whether hatred for other individuals or for other economic, social, racial, or religious groups. The intolerant propagandist school seems to me, on the balance, an evil and a dangerous thing. But it seems to me also to be a challenge and a warning.

I see this challenge and warning not only in schools under a dictatorship but in the propaganda which is invading schools in other countries as well. It is common in our day to find extremist groups of adults trying to win school children as recruits to their ranks. Communist propaganda in schools is a serious problem to the authorities in some countries; fascist or other ultra-right-wing or ultra-nationalist activity in others. These forms of propaganda are effective because they appeal to the same motive that education appeals to in the dictatorship countries. I do not know the situation in England, so I cannot be thought to allude to anything in this country in this respect. But I would like to say in passing that besides the propaganda of most extremist groups— propaganda that stands condemned because it seeks to inculcate hatred—there are at the present time certain forms of propaganda approved by governments and large sections of enlightened public opinion. The world is so full of trouble and its conflicts are so intense that you find people of many different camps breaking down the isolation of the schools and trying to win children for their views. That is, to my mind, partly a good thing. I like to see the isolation of the school broken down. But I also think that it is a dangerous thing. Propaganda should be recognised as such and whatever its purpose, be handled with circumspection by educationists.

The challenge which this state of affairs levels at education is serious. It is, indeed, part of a far wider challenge, that of our time. Mankind is in a parlous state. We are living under the threat of war (and it is certain that war, if it occurs, will not only rage between peoples of different states, but also between different social and economic groups within the same area—it will be civil war, the most horrible of all forms of war). We feel the foundations of society rocking: old forms of organisation are proving inadequate, and new forms are being imposed by violence and without sufficient preparation. We see on the one hand over-production, and on the other hand starvation: on the one hand a mutual interdependence of states as never before, and on the other a rising tide of hostility and re-arming. Whither is this witches' dance leading us? Certainly not to peace and serenity—the academic serenity to be attained by passing a matriculation examination.

As individual human beings, too, we have problems to meet that are difficult and pressing. We do not seem to be solving them adequately for ourselves and certainly cannot hope to hand on ready-made solutions to those that come after us. If our children are not blown to bits or poisoned before they reach manhood, they will have to find new moorings in place of the old from which their parents have cast loose. In marriage, in religion, in ethical values, they will have to make up their accounts afresh. Man is filled with a vague but intense longing. His picture has been painted in Galsworthy's "White Monkey"; the poor creature who wants something terribly badly, but does not know what it is.

The challenge to educators of our time is to meet this situation. It calls for a searching of heart and a remaking of our conception of education. I do not think it means that we should give up anything that modern education has been doing towards what may be summed up as the "development of personality in an international world". But I think it means that we must be alive to the danger of letting the individual feel that his precious personality is the be-all and end-all, the centre of the stage, the focus of our efforts. Youth should in its schools feel that it is subordinate to something bigger outside and that the purpose of the whole process is not just the development of its personality in an international world, but service in a cause. It should feel this just as vividly as youth does in schools under a dictatorship. The White Monkey wants an aim. Let us give him one: the service of mankind.

We, too, must evolve an education that will grip the young every whit as much as the propagandist school does. Let us even admit that it is difficult to draw a sharp line between education and propaganda. Propaganda is an attempt to serve some specific institution by effecting some specific change in human beings. It may under this definition take the form of spreading truth or untruth. But that is irrelevant. The point is that the institution it serves is limited in scope, and the changes it seeks to effect are specific and laid down *a priori*. It may, for instance, be true that Guinness is good for you or it may not; the attempt to persuade people that it is so nevertheless constitutes propaganda. It may be true that supporting the O.T.C. is your duty or it may not; the attempt to make you believe that it is constitutes propaganda. Whether it be true that the League of Nations is a desirable institution or not, the attempt to convince us that it is constitutes propaganda.

Education, too, is an attempt to serve an institution, but no less an institution than humanity; and education, too, seeks to effect changes in human beings to fulfil its aim, but the changes it sets out to achieve are the all-round growth of the individuals who are to serve humanity. It is, as you see, a difference of degree that separates propaganda from education—but an important difference. I think I am right, under my definition, in calling the function of the school for citizenship education rather than propaganda. In so doing, I have parted company with the cloistered "neutral" school, but equally with the propaganda school with its ready-made programme, its narrow appeal, and its premium on strong feeling and weak thinking.

Let us begin by acknowledging the difficulty of our position. We have not, as the propagandists have, a specific and detailed programme to offer, with achievement just around the corner, and uniforms, secret signals, and flags to enliven the march. The more immediate and limited the aim, the easier it is to make it vivid and appealing to an immature mind; the more exclusive and persecuted the group, the easier it is to win for it discipline and loyalty—and the more difficult it is to obtain clear or independent judgment; but that is not a consideration that worries the propagandists. We have therefore at the outset two handicaps: the remoteness of our aim, which is no narrower than civilisation, and our method, which is not to offer a ready programme, but to develop informed and independent thought. The difficulty of our task is, however, no reason for abandoning it. It is a reason for surveying it and setting to work.

Sir Ernest Simon sums up the aims of education for citizenship under four heads:

1. A sense of social responsibility,

2. A love of truth and freedom,

3. The power of clear thinking in everyday affairs,

4. A knowledge of the broad political and economic facts of the modern world.

Two of these desiderata are emotional and the other two are intellectual. I should like to add a fifth—practical ability in the duties and tasks of citizenship, achieved through actual experience. Thus, the aims of education for citizenship are threefold—emotional, intellectual and practical.

Let us take the intellectual and practical problem first. I admit that emotion is primary and intellect secondary, yet the latter is of great importance too. Intelligence is not to be dismissed as a mere non-Aryan invention. We wish to develop independent judgment, the inquiring attitude of mind, questioning not for the sake of being in opposition, but as a means of seeking the truth. This aim brings us in sharp opposition to dictatorial education. Dictatorships are full of matters too holy for inquiry (the collective state, the corporate state, the Aryan race, national honour, etc., etc.). To my mind there are no matters too holy to be discussed and studied by the inquiring intellect, particularly by an intellect rendered by experience aware of its own limitations.

The intellect, however, is not developed *in vacuo*. Bertrand Russell has somewhere said: "It is impossible to develop intelligence without acquiring knowledge. The opposite is unfortunately possible." The truth in this statement brings us face to face with the problem of the *content* of our education, i.e. of the curriculum.

Let us for a moment forget that there are accepted school subjects and ask ourselves what facts, what ideas, what activities are of sufficient importance to the growing generation to be included in our curriculum.

Here I think we shall do well to be guided by what I called in my lecture yesterday the Here and Now principle. Let us start in the primary stage with trying to give the child an understanding of its immediate surroundings and its daily life: with the purely geographical surroundings, the population, buildings, means of transport, food supply, industries of the locality, and the study of how people live, of wages and family budgets, of social institutions and local history. The way has been shown by many pioneers, notably by Decroly. Books have their place, but the immediate source of knowledge in the primary stage should be first-hand. Material and observations gathered on excursions, interviews with workers in different spheres, publications issued by various institutions—these constitute the first and most essential textbooks. Such material also forms the best starting point for the creative imagination, while the summaries, descriptions, diagrams, tables, the drawing of conclusions, and making of generalisations afford practice in number and language work.

In the secondary stage of education the central topic of the curriculum should be an expansion of the material indicated above: e.g. studies of the organisation of community life, of taxation and community finance, of local and central government, of the budgets of social institutions, of the organisation of industries, banks, publishing enterprises, of industrial and agricultural processes. Through association in time and space (how are similar things done elsewhere? how was this done before and how has it come to be thus?), a geographical and historical background can be built up until a good grasp of our world to-day and yesterday has been given.

An intelligent and informed interest in the political, social and economic problems of the day seem to me to form the crown of education for citizenship. The school should therefore include controversial topics among its subject-matter.

How then are we to avoid the prejudging of issues by the teacher? No matter how earnestly he strives to make his presentation of a topic objective, his bias will surely show itself—if in no other way than at least through the facts he selects for emphasis and those he leaves out because he regards them as unimportant. One way of solving the difficulty is to call in different authorities and let them argue their case before the children. I think there is much to be said for an occasional use of this method. We want, however, the younger generation not merely to listen to the discussion of controversial topics, we want them to study these topics and to discuss them for themselves. In my experience they are most likely to do so when grown-ups do not take part in the discussion.

For some years now I have been experimenting with "current events" classes in the school where I am employed. We draw our subject-matter chiefly from the daily papers, and I generally start the class by asking its members which of the matters they have seen mentioned they would like to know about in further detail. When, as frequently happens in the higher part of the school, the questions asked must be regarded as controversial, I do not contribute to the discussion at all. Those who have some introductory information or opinions to give, do so, and then a date is set for the discussion proper. This takes the form either of a debate or of a series of reports representing different points of view. There are always at least four (more frequently six) set speakers. They gather their material partly from persons whom they interview, but chiefly from periodicals and the daily press, both local and foreign. My function is to act as secretary and summarise as tersely as possible on the blackboard the arguments of each speaker. I also allow myself comments on the technique of discussion and impressions of the discussion after it has terminated. Otherwise, I take no part and I consider that I have filled my function well when both parties believe me to be secretly on their side. It is not always easy to refrain from setting things to rights according to my opinions; but I do refrain and I console myself with the thought that the point of the whole activity is not that the youthful participants should arrive at the right conclusions on any given issue, but that they should be trained in the technique of gathering and considering information, and interested in the affairs of their world. They will then, I hope, be more likely to arrive at the right conclusions when they become adult.

By way of illustration I may mention the following topics among those which have been discussed in one class during the past year: protection of home industries, re-introducing the death penalty into Finland, the admission of Russia to the League of Nations, the Hitler régime, the Italo-Abyssinian question.

The method outlined above carries with it a danger of encouraging precocious and irresponsible judgments on the affairs of the adult world. If we realise this danger, I think we shall find methods of averting it. A suitably framed question, a note of doubt, an indication of aspects of the problem that have been omitted by the speakers, these and other ways an alert teacher will find to restrain the youthful Daniels from being too precipitate with their judgments. The best single method is, however, that of confronting theory with practice. The school itself should be a living community, as four-square with real life as possible, where the youthful members can have abundant opportunity of practising as well as discussing citizenship.

Certain institutions in the school are commonly in the hands of the children of to-day: e.g. games, prefectship, the editing of the school magazine. To these I should like to see added the school stationery shop and book-shop, the school bank, the library, (in day schools) the school lunch, the lost property office, the staff work of organising excursions, the school museum, a share in the care of the school grounds and, generally speaking, as much as possible of all that goes to make up the life of the school and does not require expert knowledge. Some of these enterprises will be self-supporting or even give a profit (e.g. the stationery shop), some will require an annual grant (e.g. the library), but all should be run on a budget as *bona fide* business undertakings.

I have seen every one of the activities mentioned above in actual operation and have several years' experience of the working of some of them, and I am convinced of their value in education for citizenship. They provide direct business contact with similar undertakings in the world outside, they furnish material for study in the ordinary school subjects as well as in social sciences, they make tangible and comprehensible terms and problems such as capital, turn-over, overhead, wages and dividends, assets and liabilities. They give training in co-operation and practice in electing the right man to the right post. Perhaps most important of all, they establish certain values through the medium of first-hand experience. Reliability, responsibility, courtesy, efficiency, and adaptability show themselves for what they are: essential virtues in corporate life. Proclaim themselves, indeed, in no uncertain terms; for their presence spells smooth running, successful enterprises, and a contented community; while their absence makes for experiences as painful as they are salutary.

The knowledge gained by the studies and activities of the Here and Now method is variegated and easily becomes chaotic. Some means is required to bring order into the confusion; indeed an organised survey of the school course is a crying need in all schools to-day. We have so long been accustomed to regard school studies as a close following of certain narrow lanes of knowledge that we easily forget that these lanes run through a countryside. If the rising generation is to become world-conscious and humanity-conscious, it must be given a bird's eye view of the world and of humanity. I think each school would be well employed in evolving an outline of knowledge for this purpose. To explain what I mean, and not because I hold any brief for the particular attempt made at my school, I will indicate how we are there dealing with this problem.

We have called our outline "Man and his World", which seems to me to comprise everything of which we can have knowledge. What else can we, indeed, study, other than on the one hand Man (what he is like and what he does, what he was like and what he has done); and on the other, the World (what the physical universe is like in which Man is and which he has to some extent altered, and how it has come to be that way)? In a more poetical moment, I chose the title "Man and the Garden" as less suggestive of proprietary rights and as hinting that we may even be expected to tend the garden. But that title does not go very well into Swedish (the language in which my class is working), so we left it at "Man and his World".

If we expand this title into sub-titles, I think we shall find a place for each of the accepted school subjects as well as all that we could wish to add in education for citizenship.

Let us take the World first and break that title up into three sub-headings: (*a*) the world of non-living matter (under this will come the discoveries laid bare by physics, chemistry, mineralogy, geology, meteorology, astronomy, and part of what is now studied under the name of geography); (*b*) the world of living matter (the findings of biology in its various branches); (*c*) the man-made or man-altered world (another part of the study called geography, e.g. towns, harbours, roads and railways, cultivated areas, canals and dams, factories, state boundaries, sites of government, transport systems, etc.).

The heading Man is susceptible to subdivision in many different ways. Our way was to choose as a primary subtitle "Man a psycho-physical being" (accepted studies: human zoology, psychology) and consider that our findings under this heading really would explain the whole story. Presumably, all that Man does can be explained in terms of his reactions as a psycho-physical being. This is certainly a fascinating subject for study, and our outline must be drawn up to show that it exists. While waiting for the psychologists to unravel the connecting threads, we are, however, interested in certain important secondary manifestations of the deeper lying urges of Man. It is here that the greatest variety of choice is possible. We decided to look on Man as a creative, civilisation-building creature and to ask ourselves: what main lines of activity has Man the civiliser shown himself to have most consistently pursued throughout the course of history? Or, starting from the present, what chief forms of activity do we find among our fellows, forms which on the one hand characterise the men devoted to them and on the other can be regarded as of greatest importance for civilisation?

To cut a long story short, we came to the conclusion that Man is:

(*a*) *practical* (hence activities in which the emphasis is on supplying material wants: e.g. hunting, fishing, agriculture, industry, trade, transport);

(*b*) *artistic* (hence activities in which the centre of gravity is in creative: i.e. art in all its forms);

(*c*) *social* (hence activities rendered necessary by or arising out of corporate life: e.g. languages, arithmetic, social services including education, law, politics including war, economics);

(*d*) *inquiring* (hence philosophy and all scientific research);

(*e*) *religious* (hence activities in which God-seeking and God-serving are the essentials: e.g. work in the service of a church, mission work).

These headings and sub-headings we placed on a large chart, after which we spent some profitable hours in further sub-division. If I were free to build up a course of studies as I liked, I think I should regard this chart as the curriculum. Gathering material to fill in the chart in ever greater detail would then constitute the course of studies. The work would proceed either as a kind of enlarged geography (what is the World or Man like in this or that particular and in this or that place?) or as history (how did this come about, how was it before?). I do not think it would matter if different groups of children or even different individuals made more of one part of these studies and less of some other. Obviously, no one can hope to know everything. The very existence of a summary view of the whole field would help maintain a balance and render details significant in relation to a whole.

A word of comment is perhaps still advisable. I drew up an outline like the one above more than ten years ago for myself, and when I took up the matter afresh with a class recently I had of course a picture of this early attempt in mind. I tried, however, not to lead the discussion to a foregone conclusion. We started from the question "What activities do your parents represent?" and much the same headings seemed to come tumbling out as I had drawn up before. We have courses of study rigidly determined by external requirements, so that whatever education for citizenship we achieve has to be squeezed in as an extra. I have, however, found the work on an outline of knowledge a help in linking the ordinary school studies with life and in rousing an interest in Man and the World as a whole.

I have now, in this all too long lecture, dealt with the intellectual and practical problems of education for citizenship. The emotional problem remains. I not only want the school to help in the development of informed, intelligent, and able citizens. I want it to give them a definite emotional bias, i.e. I want it to help in giving them a love of truth and freedom, and a social conscience. Love of truth and freedom is an accepted part, and has long been so, of the education that aims at "the development of personality in an international world". I need say no more about that here, save to reaffirm my allegiance. But the development of a social conscience is a demand that has become insistent only during the post-war stress.

I want to plead that this is a demand which education must heed if it is to meet the challenge of our times. Our schools must do their work in such a manner that the generations which are growing to manhood shall know not only how their fellows live, but are also moved by that knowledge, that they shall be stirred by the poverty, the injustice, and the insecurity that make life well-nigh unbearable for their fellow human beings everywhere in our world. I say advisedly our world, because we all share through our elected governments in the responsibility for its mismanagement. Unless the next generation realises this responsibility better than its elders, there is no hope for civilisation.

I am not advocating that the school should make propaganda for any specific solution of any of the specific ills that rack mankind. I am advocating that the school should seek to win youth—you may call this propaganda if you will—for the idea that every single one of them has later as a citizen to take his share of the burden, that he must think out methods of his own or at least weigh those proposed by others, and so cast his vote or bend his activities as to further the solutions he deems best. It is indifference—the indifference of the fat and greasy citizen—that not only moved the melancholy Jaques to tears, but may also find the goddess of history weeping over the wreck of civilisation.

Knowledge is necessary to awaken the social sense and to give it a useful outlet. But it is from the torch of the master that the disciple takes his fire. It is to the social conscience of the educator that we must look for the good citizen of the future. It seems hard to ask still more of the teacher than the many-sided demands already put on him by the claims of education for "the development of personality in an international world". But it is, after all, he who holds the key to the future.

Education for citizenship necessitates the social-minded educator. This does not mean that every teacher must take part in social activity or in political (beyond voting responsibly). It does, however, mean that the educator must himself be a person who is sensitive to the weal and woe of his fellows, who is socially informed, world-conscious and humanity-conscious. He must be intensely aware of the duty of a citizen in a democratic state of to-day. He himself must be filled with desire for justice and charity.

A distinguished sociologist has recently said that our times are witnessing a race between education and catastrophe. I think he is right, and I think that education has a chance of winning only if it is able, just as education under the dictatorships is, to rouse a veritable crusading spirit in the growing generation. Unlike that of the dictatorship, however, this crusading spirit must be informed by knowledge and enlightened by thought operating in freedom. And it must call youth to battle not in the service of megalomaniac nationalism, but in defence of threatened humanity.

THE PSYCHOLOGY OF THE POST-WAR BOY

H. Crichton-Miller

IF we think of the war and its effects on the present generation of schoolboys we are apt to attribute a good deal more influence to the war than is, perhaps, justifiable. Doctors hear a lot about the effect of air raids. I am tired of mothers explaining that when Peter came she was living through air raids. I have no doubt that a certain amount of harm was done as a result of ante-natal influences in the case of mothers who were undergoing acute physical fear, but it seems to me that it is exaggerated. I think that mothers who transmitted ante-natal influences to their offspring were on the whole second-rate mothers. I have seen a lot of extremely normal boys whose mothers had those experiences and who, I think, might have been influenced if their mothers had been of a neurotic character.

Also, I am inclined to think that there is a large amount of exaggeration as to the effect upon children who themselves experienced air raids. Children brought up in air-raid areas tended to be very little affected. I hear from many boys and girls that they remember being taken from their beds down to the cellar or kitchen, but the actual air-raid business is a great deal the projection of the adult mind on the child mind. We adults imagine that the bangs and crashes meant as much in terms of physical apprehension to the child as to ourselves. But it was not so.

In regard to the question of food there is also much exaggeration. The number of children who in their earlier years or months suffered from shortage of food or the rough nature of the food is very small indeed. I think this is one of the popular and rather melodramatic ways of explaining away various kinds of infirmities and deviations from the normal which are much more likely to be due to the father's temper when he came back from the war, or some emotional influence of that kind. I have not the slightest doubt that a great many of the boys you are dealing with now suffered in that way—that is to say, owing to the conditions under which their mothers lived, or the relatives to whose care they were committed lived. These people were on edge and were strained and incalculable. They were hearing about death and were anxious about their loved ones at the front. The children, therefore, suffered from the incalculability of strained tempers.

In considering the changes taking place in our social life, we must take cognisance of the psychology of the post-war boy. There are influences which have been and are progressively at work, indirectly associated with the war, which are of paramount importance in the emotional development of the boy. The first of these is the effect of the mechanisation of life. The war promoted this to a great extent. Life is becoming more a problem of the elimination of human effort. Everywhere we are learning, and our children are learning, to demand gratification without effort. We are living in a "switch-it-on" and "put-me-through" era. If a boy wants to make an assignation with a friend one hundred yards away, the first idea is not to walk that hundred yards, but to ring him up. The original idea that the telephone is there to save time is, of course, eclipsed by the idea that the telephone is there to save effort. Father may have been perfectly justified in installing the telephone originally to save his time, but now it is taken for granted that the telephone is installed to save everyone effort, including Peter. In music, we are developing into a generation of listeners instead of performers. In art, the financial reward goes to the man who can make most cameras, not to the man who can paint the best landscape. This is a big problem for us, not merely because of the extent to which our lives have become mechanised, but because of the incredibly greater extent to which this will come about in the near future. The boys you are teaching now will have a control over material things and mechanical forces far beyond our powers of imagining. We are apt to accept this without recognising that it is intimately involved with human psychology. History has afforded numberless examples of the deterioration in character that manifested itself when tribes from the north migrated to the south, when mountaineers conquered fertile plains, and when a dominant race could command unlimited slave labour. A somewhat similar change is coming over the civilised world. The satisfaction of normal desires and basic needs is becoming so easy a matter and withal more precarious than before. Mechanisation, urbanisation, and capitalism (whether state-controlled or otherwise) make man at the same time either helpless or too powerful. And either situation is less beneficial to character than the primitive one in which nature responds to human effort and enterprise by yielding the necessaries for subsistence. Effortless prosperity is nearly as detrimental to human character as penury that cannot be remedied. Closely linked to the factor of mechanisation is that of communication. With our air mails, our cables, our wireless, our press, we are living in a world of second-hand ideas. Everybody is telling us what to think, and we are bringing up our children in this atmosphere where opinions are served ready-made and ready-cooked. We live in a world in which artificial conditions of thought exist and in which to be able to think for oneself objectively without accepting the bias of another man's thought requires moral effort.

Young people recognise that their parents are living on second-hand ideas and are not really making the slightest effort to think for themselves. If they hear an argument between father and mother, it is as to whether the fellow who spoke on the wireless last night said so and so or whether the editor of such and such a paper said the opposite. Newspapers used to be the physical medium for the presentation of news. They are now something rather different, and as far as young people are concerned there can be no question that the inability to reach facts without prejudged influence is bad. They get their facts served up with opinions indissolubly associated with the facts.

The psychological outcome of all this is that you schoolmasters are dealing with, and will increasingly deal with, a generation of excessively suggestible youngsters who will take ready-made opinions much more uncritically and with much less discrimination than their fathers or grandfathers. The practical question is, Are you going to take advantage of this greater suggestibility? Are you going to see to it that they take your views on every subject uncritically, or are you going to encourage them to think for themselves and make it easy for them to argue with you?

To live in a mechanised world discourages effort. To live in a world of second-hand ideas discourages rational and reflective thought. The resultant of the two processes is a withdrawal from fulfilment and an acceptance of the principle of evasion.

A further feature of our times is the widespread occurrence of economic difficulties. Schoolmasters are constantly made aware of these. They threaten the continuity of education; they hamper the development of home life. What is the child's interpretation of economic difficulties? When father lost his job and when the Argentine dividends did not come and Michael had to be taken away from school, what was the effect of these happenings on the child? The child interprets things in terms of calculability. A stable background in life is the thing that matters most to the child. Whether a child has cake every day is relatively unimportant to him. What is of great importance is that he should be able to calculate on having cake regularly or not having it at all. When the parent has put down the deposit for a new house in a new suburb, little Christopher's mind is thrilled at the idea of moving from a flat to a house. Then the father cannot continue the instalments, and they have to move to a second-rate boarding house in Bloomsbury. The effect on the child is an impression of instability. The child begins to wonder what life is going to do to him next. These young victims of social vicissitudes are inevitably retarded in developing a wholesome feeling of herd-security. They have to learn later, more slowly and perhaps more uncertainly, that life is, in general, trustworthy. There are other circumstances of life that have fostered this sense of insecurity. Consider the number of "mobile homes" that your boys come from as opposed to the situation before the war: I refer to the father who has to do business in America for six months and takes his wife with him, leaving the boy with his grand-parents and the daughter with a maiden aunt; the official of the League of Nations and many others—in short, all the people who before the war would have maintained stable homes and now find it impossible or at least inexpedient to keep up a home for the one or two children they may have. All this spells insecurity for the child. As a race we have paid a great price for Empire in the separation involved between parents and children, but now the trouble seems to be increasing, and more and more children have makeshift homes for the holidays, with the inevitable sense of loneliness and insecurity which are engendered by such arrangements.

There is one particular aspect of this problem which arises in connection with the divided home—separated or divorced parents incur serious hardships on their children. When it has been decided in a Court of Law that a boy has to spend half his holidays with his father and the other half with his mother, the child feels inevitably that he is the victim of injustice. He may not know who is to blame, but he does know that someone has robbed him of a prerogative. And his fate is settled by adults who are often vindictive and generally unimaginative, but who invariably fall under the child's unformulated grievance, "They didn't love me enough".

And you schoolmasters have to make up to the boys the deprivations which they have suffered and are suffering. Therefore, you must be more calculable than your masters were to you. You must inspire your boys with the feeling that their own personality will always command calculable treatment from you. You may be stricter than your colleague or you may be more lenient, but the thing that counts more for these boys is that they should know where they are in relation to each adult with whom they have dealings. And, similarly, they should feel their safe status in the school community. We all know the unfortunate boy who leaves his school with no desire to see it again. We are agreed that the school has failed with that boy. I suggest that you make a census of such boys with a view to ascertaining their home background. Unless I am very much mistaken, you will find that few of them come from stable homes.

Another difficulty about the post-war conditions is the small family. How far the war had any direct bearing upon this social change need not occupy us. The fact which presents itself to you schoolmasters is that the boys you are teaching to-day have in most cases missed the advantage of belonging to large families. The consequences are twofold. First, they are less criticisable. One of the psychological truths that has come to our knowledge during the last twenty years or so, is that the child sets up an image of himself—the ego-phantasy—and that this image has taken well-nigh unchangeable form by the age of five. In the analysis of grown men we recognise time after time how slight have been the modifications effected in twenty or more years by school life and subsequent experience. Hence, one of the most critical aspects of character growth is this formation in the pre-school years of the ego-phantasy. Parents can do some good and a lot of harm; brothers and sisters can do some harm and a lot of good. The ego-phantasy of the snubbed boy leads to a genuine complex of inferiority with the probable accompaniments of compensating self-assertion and exhibitionism.

That of the spoilt boy leads to an inability to take criticism and a proclivity to take everything else. Parental valuation is one of the most essential ingredients in a well-balanced development. In large families it was regarded as such because it was shared by all. Valuation by parents of the only child tends to be misinterpreted as unreserved approval. Hence, the only child is not only self-important, but also uncriticisable. It is permissible to speculate on the effect on national character of this most critical change in the pre-school development of a new generation. One would need to believe that school and college could be counted on to work magical transformations in order to contemplate the future with optimism. But school and college work are at an impossible disadvantage which lies in the relative plasticity of the child before five as compared with the child after five. It would hardly be extravagant to predict that our present civilisation stands a good chance of being wrecked by egoism when we have a House of Commons, a Cabinet, Editors of Newspapers and so on, all only sons—or only daughters—then the nation will be at the mercy of self-important, uncriticisable egoists.

The fourth point that calls for our attention in the psychology of the post-war boy is the materialism of the social environment from which he comes. Everywhere we note the decadence of reflective thought. We are told that the pace of modern life is killing thought. Probably it would be more true to say that man can no longer keep up with the ever increasing emotional stress of life. In consequence, he retreats from feeling and seeks oblivion in a round of incessant external activities. Everyone is running away from reflection. You are dealing with a generation of boys who, long before you saw them, learned that leisure is an embarrassing commodity. Life takes on for them the aspect of a problem of distraction. They must have a ball and an implement to hit it with, a gramophone and records for it, reading matter rather than literature and a paper that tells them what they want of the news in pictures rather than in print. On every hand they have seen life being externalised and objectified. And in the face of all this you have to try to make them know themselves, to find interest in reflection, to value their own judgments, to cultivate the things of the spirit. Yet we hear that "the schoolboy of to-day is very much what his father was, and his grandfather before him". If that is true, somebody deserves great credit, for it is only too obvious that pre-school influences are definitely less favourable than they were. The schoolboy of to-day has encountered little romance, adventure, idealism. Instead he has met with some very morbid sentiment, much sensationalism, and a great deal of materialism. With such a background, a boy does not take kindly to such a high enterprise as seeking a soul of his own. They have learned from their earliest years that frustration and suffering were to be avoided at all costs. They have heard their mothers' petulant demands for an aspirin and their fathers' impatient call for a drink. Why should they renounce or endure when their parents make no effort to do either? Yet there are times for every adolescent boy when the capacity to forgo sensory gratification determines the difference between growth in self-respect and childish regression.

To sum up, then, I submit that in dealing with the post-war boy you schoolmasters of to-day have certain special difficulties to cope with. The first comes from the mechanisation of life and the increasing reluctance to make effort. The second emanates from the instability of domestic background and the consequent fear of vicissitude. The third is the result of the small family and shows itself in the self-important and uncriticisable egoist. The last is the outcome of widespread materialism that accompanies a flight from feeling and reflection. This would indeed constitute ground for pessimism were it not that the schoolmaster of to-day is in equipment, if not also in personality, definitely superior to his predecessor.

EDUCATION FOR LEISURE

T. F. Coade

OUR attitude to leisure depends on our attitude to life. Similarly, our attitude to life can often best be gauged by a scrutiny of our leisure. An illuminating paragraph from Dean Inge's *Speculum Animae* puts the matter in a nutshell:

"The rank of the individual soul, of our own self, our personality, is determined by the things we are interested in, by the things we love. What we love, that we see; and what we see, that we are. There is no escape from this law. Where our treasure is, there will our heart be also. It is of no use to fill our days with work which we consider useful, if the moment that the tension is relaxed our minds fly spontaneously to thoughts of money, ambition, self-indulgence, or some favourite frivolity. The mind is dyed the colour of its thoughts; its leisure thoughts."

What we do and what we think in leisure is, then, very closely connected with what we are.

Now the public school boy is going out into a world where there is going to be more and more leisure. We claim that public school boys are trained to be leaders. That means that they should be able to tackle with imagination and with intelligence the problems that confront them in the adult world into which they go. How can a public school boy, who has never been trained to use his own leisure, help the vast numbers of industrial and agricultural workers, employed and unemployed, to use theirs? I think it is fair to say that the industrial, if not the international peace of the future depends very largely on how schools in general tackle this problem of leisure. Nor is it simply a social problem: it is concerned with the springs of thought and action, and therefore concerns the roots of personal and communal life.

Perhaps the most important effect of scientific research and invention upon the social and international life of the present age is the rapid metamorphosis of the world from a loose patchwork into a feverish, close-knit organism, in which a disturbance in one part has immediate reactions in every other part. This change has come about suddenly—long before mankind was ready for it morally or emotionally. This, together with the rapid increase in the total number of leisure hours both for employed and, obviously, for unemployed men and women, has produced a situation of intense difficulty in less than a generation. And in spite of adjustments and temporary expedients designed to bolster up the health of the organism in this crisis, no thinking person imagines that tinkering with the symptoms will restore its health. The world needs a new kind of citizen; citizens with a new outlook and a new heart. And that result can be achieved, in modern conditions, by education alone.

What is the fundamental change of outlook necessary? In a word, it is that *the new citizen must be essentially co-operative and not competitive in his approach to private and public problems.* And he must not merely be prepared to co-operate at a crisis; he must be a *habitual* co-operator, one whose co-operative habit of life is the outcome of a philosophy of life that is born of faith and reinforced by experience from childhood upwards. This new outlook must show itself first in the will to co-operate with life, instead of resisting or fearing it (this has an important bearing on the use of leisure); second, it must show itself in the will to co-operate with our fellow-men, instead of resisting and fearing them. I have deliberately emphasised the order of these two attitudes of mind, because Englishmen more than almost any other race are in the habit of putting the cart before the horse in this matter. There can be no true or lasting co-operation with our fellow-men until we have come to terms with life, and are prepared to work with life. Where there is no co-operation with life, there can be no enduring joy. And without joy there can be no whole-hearted co-operation with other men and other nations. The order is always the same. "Thou shalt love the Lord thy God...this is the first and great commandment; and the second is like unto it: thou shalt love thy neighbour." "Glory to God in the highest; and on earth peace towards men of good will." Temporal values must always be relative to, and tested by eternal values. Or—if we interpret this in educational terms— the creed of modern education is, first, belief in the development of the individuality or personality of the child, and second, belief in training the young to be co-operative members of a group. The first belief is not necessarily more important than the second; but the second is dependent on and implicit in the first. The crying need of the world is for fully developed men. Nine-tenths of our worries are due to the prejudices of amateurs and badly educated specialists in positions of authority. It is the task of education to produce whole men whose citizenship is learnt not only from school books and sport, but from years of daily creative and co-operative experience at home and at school, in working hours and in leisure: men and women who are emotionally as well as intellectually free. It is the tremendous task and privilege of education—that is, of parents and teachers—to pave the way for the feet of the next generation and guide them into the way of peace.

The most casual observer of the modern world cannot fail to notice both in public and private life two outstanding characteristics: fear, and the absence of high or definite aim.

Let us take aimlessness first. The real difficulty at the root of our woes, at all events in this country, is that very few of us, not even the so-called leaders, know what to do next; or if they know what to do, i.e. if their reason tells them, they seem to have neither the desire nor the courage nor the ability nor the initiative to set about doing it. The commonest characteristic of individual and public life to-day is lack of aim, absence of any sense of plan or purpose. Bernard Shaw once said "to be in hell is to drift, to be in heaven is to steer". It is impossible to get the problem of personality and State-control settled on progressive lines, and even more to get nations and individuals to co-operate, where there is no sense of common purpose, and where men have lost faith in life, in themselves, and in one another.

The first task of education is to remedy this modern disease of aimlessness by removing the causes of it. The causes can best be removed in childhood and in adolescence, before they have got a proper hold, i.e. while the foundations are still being built. And it is useless to discuss the profitable use of leisure so long as life is devoid of purpose. For a sense of purpose gives that blessed and rare human quality single-mindedness. And single-mindedness gives to the man who achieves it the equally blessed sense of interior unity that comes from an intuitive knowledge of the close relationship between all that he does, especially between his work and his leisure and between both of these and his destiny—his place in the great plan or pattern of life.

We do not achieve single-mindedness until we are able to feel intuitively this relationship between everything we do and that which we were born to become. I can perhaps best illustrate my meaning by considering the attitude of the golfer when he stands at the tee. His purpose is to reach the hole with the ball. And in the act of driving he is more or less conscious all the time of the flag on the green. But his immediate and direct attention is on the ball at his feet. There must be, however, both in the golfer, and in ourselves when we face life, a conscious relationship between the immediate job in hand and the ultimate objective. And I believe there is no possibility of a joyful and purposeful life, and so no chance of attaining interior unity, without this underlying sense of the relationship between what we are doing here and now, and what we were born to become—our destiny. Is it strange that with this lack of single-mindedness, this absence of purpose in adult life, there should be a corresponding vagueness and futility about the underlying principles of education, and about the significance of leisure? The aim of education is integration. Therefore, anything that is disintegrating must be faced, and if possible got rid of, before any purpose can become clear or any unity begin to grow. Aimlessness is dissipating and disintegrating. There is only one thing more disintegrating; and that is fear, which it so often engenders.

Fear is always with us; it always has been with us. We know this, and we can see on every side evidences of the havoc it causes, notably in international relations. We long to free our children from the incubus it has laid on our own lives; and we cannot. Fear in the sense of prudence—the recognition of the inevitable result of breaking natural and spiritual laws—is a good thing. The fear we are devastated by is panic, which shows itself either in paralysis of the will resulting in incapacity for decisive action, or in flight from the dilemma, in refusal to face facts, and in the formation of the habit of escape into unreality, into a world of fantasy. Such a state of mind, which is widespread in Europe to-day, needs psychological treatment. That can be provided only by education, which must tackle the disease as early as possible—that is, in the home and in the school. Health is to be restored only by setting free into suitable and satisfying channels the life that has been dammed up by fear. This is not a digression; the subject of fear is closely concerned with the subject of leisure, because, as a rule, schools are afraid of leisure and try to solve their difficulty in the worst way, namely, by curtailing leisure. If children are to be taught the use of leisure, they must be given leisure.

This fear of leisure is one of which schools are usually unconscious; but it is there all the same. Nor is it very far below the conventional surface of school life and routine—a vague fear of what might happen if this or that habit or tradition or restriction passed out, and the new values demanded by a changing civilisation took their place. This fear is, first and foremost, fear of freedom; and it shows itself in masters as well as in boys. In masters it is fear of the essential nature of boys; and there are still many schools in which as little leisure as possible is allowed, lest evil thoughts and practices, through increased opportunity, should creep in and establish themselves. Almost everybody in the educational world fears a vacuum, not realising that without space there can be no stillness; and without stillness there can be no true growth.

This fear of leisure is contagious, and boys themselves soon begin to be afraid of what they may be tempted to do in spare time. They are in any case, during adolescence, only too easily made afraid of themselves and of life. Pressing outwards from within is life—the life more abundant, which Christ came to set free. Pressing downwards from outside is authority: not that true authority which exists to enable youth, by the flexible limits it ordains, to find fuller and richer freedom; but an authority whose policy of limitation is rigid, just because it is based on the fear of freedom.

So, from the lack of legitimate and abundant outlet, this surging tide of life is driven back on itself. And the boy in his spare time alternates between periods of bored stagnation, and periods of futile or destructive eruption. Evidence of this kind of fear is most easily recognisable in nervous habits, in the inability of so many boys to concentrate, in undue bumptiousness, in irresponsibility, in acute sexual disturbance.

The policy (or perhaps it is an instinct) of schoolmasters is not to recognise this fear of freedom, but to flee from it and erect in its place idols, to the worship of which nearly all available time and energy are dedicated. Sometimes the idol is Games, sometimes Examination Results, sometimes Specialisation. In any case, it is flight from facing the problem of leisure.

Nor is it schoolmasters alone who fear leisure: we all fear it for our children, for workers, for the unemployed—even for ourselves maybe.

Why do we fear it? Partly because it forces us to make choices; it challenges us, not to activity dictated by necessity, but to spontaneous activity—to doing something, to making something, to translating the divine creative life within us into beautiful form or fruitful action. But this creative life is itself another thing that we fear, either confusing it with mere sex activity, or shrinking from the effort involved in true creation. In other words, we are afraid of being ourselves; and we are afraid of leisure because if we face it squarely it compels us to be ourselves. The machinery of industry and the machinery of education are largely to blame for the fear of effort. Ignorance of our true natures is to blame for the fear of this creative impulse within us. And so, when the industrial age which our cleverness has created throws leisure at us, instead of welcoming it and turning it to recreative use, we are bored or frightened by it and take refuge from it in fantasy and sensationalism. At best we are content with pastimes.

Leisure is then a challenge to the boy and to the man to be himself. But mere freedom from outward authority is not enough. He must be inwardly free too if he is to use his leisure creatively. That means that in childhood and early youth he must be given an increasing amount of leisure in order to realise and be himself; he must be trained within to enable him to appreciate and use this royal road to freedom.

I would summarise the situation and problem thus. The fundamental desire of human children is to create; the fundamental (though largely unconscious) need of the human adolescent is self-discovery, self-realisation by means of creation—the process which leads to a complete adulthood and the attainment of a faith and a satisfying philosophy which make life full and significant. If this process is to follow a normal and ordered development, it matters tremendously what happens during the early stages, i.e. during the Preparatory and Public School period—the age during which scope for the human creative instinct and self-discovery are of supreme importance. In these early stages creation is a much more personal thing than is possible under the class system of teaching and the system of organised games. It finds its fullest expression in those occupations which are still unfortunately

10-2

regarded in nearly all schools as side-shows or side-tracks—music, art, crafts, literary work, drama, and the pursuits of many school clubs and societies. Many of these activities, essential to the normal child, are 'extras' at most schools, and excellence in them is not seriously recognised by school authorities or by the tradition of the boys themselves; consequently only a very limited minority practises them. Therefore, to most boys free time is apt to mean, more or less, a period of boredom; it is seldom long enough to settle down to anything interesting. In any case such occupations as have been suggested demand more freshness and more effort than are available at the end of a hard day of class-work and organised play. It is easier to read a magazine, or 'rag about', or turn on the wireless.

And yet, though boys are often unconscious of it, this creative imaginative work is what the vast majority of them feel the need of above all else. These creative leisure activities give several things which cannot otherwise be obtained. First, they give opportunity for private employment, individual expansion, solitude when the boy can think or feel undisturbed by, and unaware of, the scrutiny of the critical, and the noise of the indifferent; they make silence and solitude things to be loved, not to be dreaded. Secondly, they give the opportunity for practising concentration spontaneously—a faculty which I believe can be transferred, once it is acquired by constant practice, to other less engrossing subjects. Thirdly, they give the boy a chance of cultivating wider interests, developing new faculties, intellectual, imaginative, and manual, which will open up to him a varied field of happy constructive employment in his leisure later on. And if the provision of time for such occupations involves the reconstruction of the time-table, even if it involves the scrapping of outworn educational machinery and the transformation of the public examination system, it is a thousand times worth while.

There are practical difficulties in the way of reform, but I believe none of these to be insuperable, once the fundamental importance of the necessity of training future citizens for leisure is grasped.

Schools which do make time and opportunities for leisure and for this kind of employment very soon notice two things: first, the growth of a new refinement showing itself in a progressive decrease of horseplay, coarseness, and hooliganism. Next, and more gradually, there is apparent an easing of the sexual tension that is otherwise present in all schools for adolescents. The connection betweeen creative leisure activities, especially manual activities, and the problems of puberty is very close. Sex itself is a creative instinct. Where plenty of happy creative leisure occupation is available, the sex instinct naturally dominant at puberty and in adolescence, instead of being acutely concentrated on self, is to a large extent diffused or sublimated in more productive employment.

It is along these lines that the approach to reality, for most children, lies. When these fields of experience are denied, a situation arises such as one can see on every side to-day in adult life. Unable to find joy or adventure in themselves, the vast bulk of the population, young and old, seeks it exclusively in the many forms of 'distraction' provided by the financiers and business men who control the more sensational press and public entertainments. That is why second-class cinemas are full; that is why the less reputable press runs into millions of copies every day, that is why horse-racecourses, dog-racing tracks, dirt tracks, and professional football grounds are crammed. They are filled with and patronised by people who, finding nothing in themselves, are desperately seeking for second-hand sensations outside themselves. Along with this goes the whole psychology of shirking life, of escaping facts rather than facing them, of living in a day-dream, in a fantasy world, that produces nothing durable—only emptiness, hunger, and regret.

Such use (or abuse) of leisure acts as all drugs act; it generates an ever-growing craving for more. And it is mainly negative. The leisure that truly liberates the spirit must be positive (i.e.

it must be related to some standard and some purpose). It does not matter so much what we do, as whether we do it negatively or positively, whether we make contact with reality, or are trying to flee from it.

In places where the leisure problem is tackled in a bold and liberal spirit, a new quality is generated, which one might call 'naturalness'. But training for leisure is something more—it is training to be one's self, to be real—which is more than to be natural. What is a real person? Someone more positive than a merely natural person. Someone who, when freed from activity dictated by outer necessity, uses his active leisure most often in one of two ways, according as the spirit moves him. Either he uses it in the act of direct creation, e.g. in art, drama, music, building, modelling, writing, constructive thought; or he uses it in what might be called 'positive receptivity', e.g. in the enjoyment or contemplation of all things which enable boy or man, in the words of Henry Vaughan, to feel

> ..."through all this fleshly dress,
> Bright shoots of everlastingness".

This faculty of creative receptivity can equally well be called 'responsiveness'—responsiveness to the sounds and sights of nature, to the majesty or the grace of form in mountains and trees; to the miracle of light on clouds or water; to the universal law of rhythm in the song of birds, in the ebb and flow of the tides and the return, after winter, of spring; responsiveness, too, to the intense joy and fierce pain that attend the birth of all great works of art, the responsiveness of something immature, but none the less divinely creative within ourselves, if we are truly alive, to that same creative power expressing itself through the mind of the musician, the artist, the scientist, the engineer.

In the practice of this creative receptivity in leisure there is one human faculty which almost more than any other needs training in this age of tension and rush, if leisure is to have the truly recreating influence it should—I mean the faculty of loosening the tension of the body and mind so that, as a depleted battery is recharged, the soul may literally be restored, re-created, by contact with the regenerating power of God. The boy who takes the trouble to learn relaxation is, I believe, on a quicker and surer road to learning the art of prayer than we realise.

This brings us not very far from responsiveness to the highest art of all, responsiveness to the supreme artist in living, the incarnation of the full and abundant life of the Creator Spirit—and so to religion.

The connection between leisure and religion, as between work and religion, is in this peculiarly human, or rather divine, faculty of creation. The recognition of this fact in connection with the religion of children and adolescents is quite imperative, if their religion is to become real and personal. Surely the aspect of God which children first come to understand is that of God the Creator. From the very earliest years that which brings fullest joy to children is making things; and this is mainly an emotional experience. Creation in children is a real though barely conscious experience of unity with the Creator Spirit, by whom we ourselves are created. When a child is completely engrossed in, e.g., making a story, a poem, a picture, a boat, a model, he is probably enjoying the highest religious experience of which he is capable at that age. And it is because we never allow him to know that, but rather allow him to think of religion as a matter mainly of formal prayers and services, that the most vital and significant experiences of his life come to be regarded by him as having nothing whatever to do with religion or with God.

If the child or adolescent can come to understand that when he is engaged in creative work of any kind he is, within the limits of his own nature, working with God, acting as the channel through which the Creator Spirit is finding expression, and that he is therefore in his own small way helping in the evolutionary plan of which he is a part, that he is actually learning how to live—then life can take on a new meaning and religion begins to be real to him. This is not the whole of religion to the child, but it is an integral part of it which is usually neglected or forgotten at school. Unless a boy can feel something of this sense of purposeful creative joy in all that he does, in his games, in his physical training, in all his leisure activities and in his work—however strenuous or laborious this may be—these pursuits are bound to become increasingly meaningless, and life therefore begins infallibly to lose significance.

I cannot think of a better conclusion to this paper than a statement on this very subject by Dr A. A. David, Bishop of Liverpool:

"It is often said that religion is 'caught not taught'. Some go further and declare that 'nothing can be taught—all the teacher can do is to show that there are paths'. In each of these sayings there is as much truth as an epigram can be expected to contain. The undeveloped religious sense, latent in every child, grows best by contact with those in whom it is already growing. And the boy must indeed seek his own path. But to find it he needs the light that shines through human experience of God. This can come to him only through teaching. But it is a mistake to suppose that teaching is going to make him religious. He is religious already. His response to God above him and around him is being made in terms of life as he sees life. He cannot express it in a form easily intelligible to us, nor can we analyse it. But we can discern it and help it to grow. And in this process we must recognise that collects and hymns and statements of doctrine intended for the adult mind will seldom be of much immediate use to him. He can indeed be alive to the beauty of their language. But much of the truth so enshrined belongs to a life which he has not yet attained. By anticipating it, they may repel him rather than attract. And they can never be quite real to him till a growing experience enables him to fill them with a content of his own."

LEADERSHIP

Sir Robert Waley Cohen

Brains and character, the elusive quality of 'flair', a strong
constructive sense, the personal qualities of loyalty and
courage which enable a man both to work with his fellows
and to persuade them to work with him, are essential elements
in all leadership, and if commercial instinct be added and a
sense of the high purpose which the creation of wealth must
serve in the world of our generation, you have almost a
complete catalogue of the qualities necessary to make a leader
in commerce and industry to-day.

It is a simple picture, and yet it is not always easy to identify.

Most of those responsible for the restaffing of commerce
and industry after the war must have encountered the former
member of H.M. Forces, who, when applying for a post in
commerce or industry and deprecating his lack of any special
qualifications, generally added "but of course my training has
been that of a leader of men, and if you want that I am your
man". Such men have usually been mere cogs in a machine,
armed with an iron discipline in respect of their fellows, em-
powered to demand or required to render unquestioning
obedience. The instrument by which their duty has been
fulfilled bears, of course, no resemblance to the elastic and
elusive quality of leadership. It is the powerful and rigid
machine of discipline: if it were an adequate substitute for the
quality of leadership how easy would be the task of finding
leaders in commerce and industry. And yet the man who
possesses that quality is generally strikingly indifferent to and
independent of the forces of discipline. He knows how to
obey when, as must frequently occur in the course of his
career while a subordinate, his movements are controlled by
forces which lie outside his knowledge or experience. But

with a mind at all times alert to grasp the principles which control the events around him, he will not be long in forming sound judgments, and, by means of them, conditioning his daily tasks. Thus, early in his career there will emerge the priceless quality of initiative for which leaders in commerce and industry are always on the look-out.

Unlike a military unit, a commercial unit must always be elastic: a junior who has shown the grasp of principle and the power to form a sound judgment as to how practical improvements may be initiated and intelligence in applying them, will at once be accorded a lead by his contemporaries. Thus it is that where there is good leadership at the top of a business there is always scope for leadership at the bottom. And this is perhaps one of the fundamental things which enables the large units of commerce and industry which are characteristic of the present age to attract and to offer to the best type of boy from the top of a public school a career worthy of his steel. If he possesses high qualities of mind and intelligence, these have been developed and trained by scholars with a high standard: his powers of human co-operation have been brought out and encouraged by the unique system of social education which a very precious tradition has made the peculiar inheritance of our great public schools. If a boy is to be a leader in commerce and industry, his qualities of intellect must, as soon as he has mastered routine, show themselves in the possession of creative imagination, of the ability to see beyond the current daily tasks of detail which absorb the humbler mind.

A leader in commerce and industry must be able to direct his own mind and that of his staff to working out those new developments which are constantly demanded by the advance of knowledge and without which no commercial enterprise can live. An example of this may perhaps best be found in the classic case of the failure by the coal industry to utilise Professor Perkins' famous discovery of aniline dyes. The managers of the coal industry in those days were mostly not educated men, and in any case education in England was so devoid of any scientific basis that the captains of the coal industry were not capable of conversing intelligently with scientific men about their work, and they were entirely unable to utilise the new discovery. The result was that a great source of latent wealth discovered in England had to be transferred to Germany before it could be made available to mankind, while the English coal industry suffered a steady decline and is still feeling the effects of that fatal deficiency.

The intellectual problems are not always of such dramatic importance, but the great units of commerce and industry of the present day demand of their leaders at every turn the power to grasp new problems which are constantly brought to them by those who are responsible for conducting the various parts of these great organisations. To respond to that call, a man must be able to bring to bear upon these problems not only a grasp of general principle, but also an alert understanding of the special problems themselves, so that in comparatively short and rare conversations the men who are responsible for the progress of the enterprise as a whole may give to the leaders of each part both the guidance of their wider outlook and the stimulus of their creative insight, sending them away with a sense that they have been given a lead in the solution of their existing problems and a direction in thinking out lines of further progress. No head of a great commercial or industrial organisation can find time to make a detailed study of all the factors which must contribute to his decisions. He must possess a quick and intuitive brain so that in the course of comparatively short and rare conversations with his staff he may be able to form a rapid grasp of minor problems and take decisions which, in a sufficiently large proportion of instances, must be right, notwithstanding his necessary inability to study all the details by which the problems are conditioned. Some of those who have been successful leaders of smaller units fail in this respect to compass the management of the large units of to-day. In their own comparatively simple tasks men controlling what may perhaps have been a 'good family business' were able to make a prolonged and exact study of every question on which they were called upon to take a decision. That opportunity is denied to the leader of a modern business, who, if he lacks the quality of 'flair', will be submerged in the endeavour to study masses of details and will not be found competent to handle the wide range of exacting tasks for which he must be ultimately responsible and on the successful fulfilment of which will depend the success and, in the end, the survival of the business.

It is in these brief interviews with his staff, which constitute so large a part of the life of a leader in a great business, that his human qualities are put to the test. He must be a sufficient judge of character to be able to form, in these meetings, an opinion as to the power of his departmental manager to grapple with the difficulties of his department; to initiate progress on the limited scale; and to absorb his leader's guidance in such a way as to make the progress of his unit converge with that of others of the group. Judgment in appreciating his staff, which can only wisely be based on intercourse of this kind and not merely on a study of results, will determine in a very large measure the success of the leader of a great business, for no truth comes home to him more rapidly than his own inability to achieve anything without the co-operation of an efficient team of alert intelligent staff running through the whole organisation. In these human relations the leader receives as well as gives. He is always dependent on those of his staff who are in closer contact with the consuming public than he can hope to be.

It is one of the main functions of the head of a great business to bear the public interest constantly in mind. A small unit, whose success or failure is conditioned by the stresses of competition, can succeed by the mere process of outwitting its competitor. But the leader of a large business, stimulated by intercourse with men constantly looking up to him to initiate the direction of progress, if he is tempted by some apparent immediate advantage to allow his industry to run counter to the public interest, will before long find himself opposed by the force of public opinion to which a great industry is far more sensitive than a small competitive unit. This does not, of course, mean that he should cultivate in any sense the political mentality, the capacity of conforming to a popular current of the time. It is, in fact, an expansion in terms of leadership of the power of salesmanship to the larger sphere in which to-day a leader of a great industry operates. In essence the task of the salesman is to discover how he can serve the real requirements of his customer, so that, if he persuades a buyer to take his goods or his service, the buyer will find that in doing so he has rendered himself a service. The customers of a great industry are the public, and one of its main problems is to acquire and retain the goodwill of the public by constantly serving its interests. It is one of the main functions of the leader to keep his mind on these large issues and to impress their implication upon the managers.

I have tried to indicate how exacting are the demands of leadership in commerce and industry to-day, and in doing so I have perhaps suggested the importance of one other quality of leadership in these large tasks which I have not so far mentioned, viz. the power of a man who possesses all these qualities to subordinate his whole life to the requirements of his exacting task. It demands a man's whole mind and thought and will not brook dilution. The call of affairs which loom more attractively in public esteem than the direction and control of a great business has sometimes led men to weaken in their devotion to its service. In public affairs responsibility may be shared with Boards or Committees, but leadership in commerce demands personal responsibility, and with it a readiness to give credit for the success of subordinates and to observe the loyalty which alone can command and stimulate the co-operation of the large numbers of those who must share the burden. Personal ambition will receive its meed of satisfaction in the public esteem which successful achievement in this field is beginning to command. In any other form it is a weakness which brings disaster in its train.

The public school spirit has been so well expressed in the course of your meetings that I will not presume to embark upon the same theme, but if any schoolmaster has cared to read these notes on the qualities which are demanded of the leaders of the great units to which commerce and industry are tending in modern times, I feel sure he must have felt how particularly well fitted is the English tradition in education to develop those qualities if the right raw material is there to start with. By the process of competition which applies to every activity in a public school there emerge at the top of the school boys who possess the qualities of intellect and character which are essential to those whom the country requires to lead us back to our place in the forefront of the world's commerce and industry, and by the education in fellowship and public spirit which runs through every stage of the career of a boy at a public school the boys whose characters are capable of being expanded into those of a leader receive the highest possible development. Practised in the exercise of team work, in the subordination of personal interests to those of their house and their school, they are taught as by no other system to accept and exercise responsibility and initiative, and in every school worthy of a place in the English educational tradition, to fulfil all these functions with a high purpose and without deviating from a rigid and exacting code of public spirit.

In the foregoing pages much space has been given to the qualities demanded of the leader who is to rise to the head of a great industry and lead it to success. But, as I explained earlier in these notes, leadership in some measure is demanded at almost every stage throughout a well-managed, active, commercial organisation. Englishmen are disinclined to subordinate their individual initiative to controlled machinery such as that by which some of the large continental enterprises are managed, but by utilising in the best way the qualities which our public schools have made characteristic of the nation, we have the opportunity of making in our great commercial enterprises not machines in which there is no room for individual freedom and initiative, but elastic bodies in which every individual from the top almost to the bottom can be given some sense of responsibility for the success of the whole and some power in helping it to meet the constantly changing taste and requirements of the public.

In the past the qualities developed in the public schools have been mainly devoted to evolving leaders for the army, the professions, and the direct service of the State. But everyone realises that at this moment in our history the problems of the creation of wealth make the more insistent claim upon the men who are to lead the world back to prosperity. The public schools, with all their fine traditions, can be and should be utilised no less effectively to produce leaders who will meet the new demand. In the period which followed the industrial revolution, when the creation of wealth was a comparatively easy occupation, and its distribution and wise use in the interests of the State demanded high qualities of mind and character, the public school boy supplied the demand. There is every reason to expect that the same type of boy, subjected to the same influences, should answer with equal distinction the new call. Fundamentally, I suppose, this tradition of the public schools was created largely by the classical master, the man whose whole life was steeped in the tradition of an heroic age. These pages may, I hope, convince some such man that the hard toil and the high purpose of the life of a modern leader in commerce and industry offers a scope not less worthy of his ablest and best pupils, a field for leadership into which they must enter if they are, at this period in our history, to serve the highest interests of the State. They must enter it not with the old sense that they are suffering a fall in moral status when they accept a humble position in a 'money-making' concern, but with the determination to apply to the daily problems of their work those principles of 'moral vigour' by which they have learnt to be guided in their lives at school. It is surely a fine expression of the qualities of courage and leadership in the present stage of civilisation for a man to thrust himself into the struggles of commerce and industry by which the nation's stature can be enlarged and its standard of living raised, rather than to seek a quiet protected life behind the battle line, merely regulating and distributing the spoils won by the adventurous spirits.

And so I will bring these notes to an end with an appeal to the public school masters to consider how they may lead the best of their pupils to go out into the exacting field of commerce and industry with an inspiration in their lives not in any way inferior, and indeed perhaps even superior, to that which was claimed by the generation who felt that it was upon the playing fields of their public schools that their military battles were won.

PERSONAL RELIGION

Geoffrey Allen

"THE development of personality in an international world." The phrase points to the most pressing issue of the present hour. We have learnt in Christ to regard personality as the central place of the self-revelation of God. In the present international world, very much that is of central value in personality is denied or called in question.

For a large proportion of the world, economic distress makes fulness of personal life impossible. For another large section, the individual is made the slave of mechanised industry; the greater part of his time is employed in work which fails to use the nobler elements in his character, and which virtually turns him into one part of the machinery he tends. The threatened break-down of economic organisation is leading inevitably to a growing centralisation of authority and control. In different forms in Germany and Italy and Russia and America, the central government is finding it necessary to centralise power in its own hands. There is danger then, that in freeing the individual from slavery to the machine, we merely make him the slave of the State. In other more subtle ways, the crowd threatens to capture and repress the individual. We ourselves, with our legacy of freedom of thought, are not exempt from the tendency toward the spread of a communal mass mind. Popular press and cinemas and broadcasting may become ready instruments for the spread of a uniform type of mentality, and a type not always close to the Mind of Christ.

Probably this centralisation of authority in the realm of economic organisation will continue; certainly by some means we must press forward for a solution of the denial of the rights of personality in unemployment. We must, how-

LHL   11

ever, beware that with this centralisation, other more precious gifts are not thereby frustrated and denied. You cannot centralise or command genius; the birth of genius requires freedom of movement for the Spirit in the individual soul. It is symptomatic of the times that in Germany artists as well as clergy have found themselves driven into protest against the totalitarian State. Similarly, learning has to become incarnate in individual minds. The advance in learning has to come as a free act of the individual; it does not flourish under the pressure of authority. The advance into truth has to pass by roads of experiment and doubt; if the pressure of a community mind checks this liberty to doubt, it will also check the forward movement into learning. Moreover, we shall find within our hearts forces which are all too ready to yield at this point. In our bewilderment, we have lost trust in the powers of rational enquiry. He therefore who speaks with authority is greeted as a liberator, delivering us from our perplexity of mind. We do not always ask whether loudness of speech is necessarily a sign of truth and accuracy of speech. Most deeply of all, religion has to become incarnate in the individual. Christianity preserves a proper balance between individual and corporate activity. Here is one of its central paradoxes. Essentially, it is the religion of fellowship; that fellowship is, however, founded in the counsel, "Thou, when thou prayest, enter into thy chamber and shut thy door." It is a central condemnation of our present crowded living that very many who dwell in cities have no secret chamber, where they can find peace alone with God.

The development of personality in a world of this kind is our central problem; and the subject of this address, "Personal religion", takes us into the heart of that problem. The development of personality cannot be made an end in itself; like other precious things in life, it comes as a bye-product, when we are seeking another purpose. Here lies the fallacy in the communist solution for our problem. Communism is not purely material; there is a genuine quest for fulness of life in the spiritual as in the material field; this quest is, however, carried out purely on the plane of the present world order, as an end to be pursued directly for its own sake. The Christian answer is psychologically more sound, that man develops himself in seeking an end beyond himself; self-development is not denied in Christianity, but it is found in the love of God. It is in the quest for a truth which has so far eluded us that we find that life acquires a new dignity and purpose. Life becomes worth while when we feel that our personality is caught up in the service of something beyond itself. "Blessed are they that hunger and thirst after righteousness, for they shall be filled"; this hunger and this fulfilment are both abiding notes of Christian experience. In religion, as in all learning, the more we acquire insight and understanding, the more do we grow into humility; we learn how far the vision before us transcends our present knowledge. I am inclined to think we have become a little over-occupied with religious experience these days. Religion does not begin nor end with ourselves. True religion begins: "Our Father, which art in heaven"— beyond all things earthly, beyond ourselves—"Hallowed be thy name". It ends: "Thine is the Kingdom and the power and the glory". It is the central task of education to place all learning in this setting. Education is a far bigger thing than the imparting of knowledge. It is the attempt to impart perspective, the point of view from which various realms of knowledge are best regarded. And this point of perspective is the point whence God from heaven regards His family and His world on earth.

It is urgent for the development of personality, that we should learn to worship; having said this, we may then say that it is even more urgent to worship the true God. There can no greater evil happen to man or society, than that we should take the name of God in vain, and use His name for something less than God. Let us look at one or two of the ways in which we do this. Mammon! We are just beginning to realise how vast and corrupting a part the money motive plays in private and social life. In the shock of that realisation, we react against it. We then forget the other side, that Christ said: "Make to yourselves friends of the mammon of unrighteousness". It is a very strange saying, but He said it! We have got to learn how to use possessions, without letting them enslave our souls; and we are very far indeed as yet from having learnt that lesson. The State! We are faced in the world with the menace of the State idolising itself, and setting itself upon the throne of God. The new State claims from its members an absolute loyalty. It receives from its members sometimes a fervid, fanatical enthusiasm. Enthusiasm is all too often built up, at the expense of reason and objectivity of judgment; we achieve enthusiasm by sweeping out of our vision facts which disturb the security of our theories. Worse still, there is the prospect of a clash, when a State which idolises itself comes into conflict with another State claiming from its members a like idolatry. Public opinion! Which of us dare say that we are not in one form or another the slave of that idol? Our personalities become mirrors of society, reflecting back at the world the phrases and slogans of the particular society in which we happen to move. In these and other ways we give our souls to something less than God. It follows that our souls are fed on insufficient food and starved. Only two courses lie open. Either we become fanatical, and enforce our opinions with persecuting power upon others, to conceal from our hearts the fact that we no longer believe in them ourselves; or else we must pass through disillusionment, when for long hours the gods torment us, whom once we have loved and now can no longer serve. It was not without reason that that first most simple, most beautiful Christian writer warned his readers, "Little children, keep yourselves from idols!"

God is Creator and Father! Here is the central doctrine we need to hear, alike for our own soul's health and for the peace of the world. Let us look for a moment at some of its implications. God is Lord of men and women. Male and female created He them and called them good. Shame over sex does not belong to the Christian faith: it belongs to the fallen world; and it is the task of the educator, to teach men to accept the order of creation, and to overcome this shame. God is the Lord of all nations. Here and here alone lies the answer for the menace of the rising tide of nationalism. We may rightly cherish the traditions of our own nation, but we may do so only if we see these traditions in terms of service for the whole family of men. God is the Lord of all religious movements. Here also there is a most necessary lesson. The Church will only have an answer for the rivalries of national-ism when she herself faces the scandal of disunion and hears herself the message she proclaims to others: "The Lord your God is One". God is Father of the individual, regarding each member of His family with all that we know and more of the most perfect human father's care. Here lies the answer for that timidity of heart, and that flight from reason, which is a characteristic of the present world. We need not, we should not mortify ourselves in the presence of God. Breaking through the timidity of our hearts there comes the message that our thought, our decision, our action, our personality, amazing though it be, have infinite value in the sight of Almighty God.

God is revealed in the tender pity of Christ! Here is the heart of the Christian proclamation. When we accept it in faith, there comes here the central moment in Christian religious experience. We come before God with thoughts of shame and weakness and failure. We let these thoughts flow into our mind in concrete detail in His presence. In Christ we hear the word spoken to our hearts, that nevertheless He loves. Life acquires a new insight, a new power of sympathy, as day by day we let this happen, and let His Spirit of Love invade all the dark corners of our hearts. Here most of all there is in Christianity a message which is intensely individual. The need of each individual is different; Christ comes to each individual with a unique love, meeting that need. We need no longer shrink from life in morbid self-abasement. Because of the promise of the Gospel, we dare to rise from our knees and take upon our lips those two first words of every Christian's Creed, "I believe...".

"Thou shalt love the Lord thy God with all thy heart and all thy mind and all thy soul and all thy strength." Each individual is called into this direct relationship of love toward God. Our response to the commandment will mean daily time set apart alone in the presence of God; it will mean through such time apart a growing practice of the presence of God throughout the day. It is a very valuable practice to turn toward God in meditation with our first waking thoughts. As we learn to do so, we shall find that our mind after sleep presents to us areas where our thought was muddled, or memories of shame and failure, or memories of work to be done. We offer these waking thoughts to God in a time of deliberate reflection; we find that He gives to our minds new clarity and new purpose, at those places where next we needed to grow. Almost we may say that sleep itself has become a kind of prayer, a time of rest and refreshment in the presence and mercy of God.

Let us bring into our prayers all the details of our daily work, and the people amongst whom we move. No detail of the created world is irrelevant to the Creator. Our lives will acquire a new calm and a new orderliness, as we learn to sanctify our work, by reflecting upon it in the presence of God. Our inmost motives and intentions are to be given to God. Christ traces every evil act to its root in evil intention. He who has begun to be irritable has begun to break the law of murder. We face our evil thoughts in the light of His forgiveness, and day by day He grants a new calm love to our souls. We are to love God each with our own mind. It is not His will that we should repeat second-hand slogans and party catch-cries; it is His will that we should use our own powers of observation and judgment, and learn to think for ourselves. In prayer we shall therefore also learn to love God with our minds. We face the figure and the words of Christ; step by step we bring all our understanding of the world, and of our own part in it, into keeping with the central purpose, that the love of Christ may reign.

"Thou shalt love thy neighbour as thyself." Our neighbour is to be seen, as a person who also has to receive the love of God and give himself in love to God. The destiny for which his soul was made was not to be the slave of the State or of machinery or of public opinion or of ourselves; it was to become a lover of God, now and through all eternity. Let those who teach learn to see each individual pupil in the setting of eternity. We have a long way to go in learning how really to awaken in other people the love of God. As I see people coming from the schools to the university, I sometimes feel how little they have learnt to pursue the quest for truth for its own sake, how little the hunger and thirst for righteousness is as yet present in their hearts, how little they have grown into fearless freedom and initiative. I am sure we must learn to see that the purpose of education is not to impart knowledge, but rather to awaken in other people the desire for knowledge. We have to give to other people the sense that God really needs from them the enquiry of their minds and the love of their hearts. Similarly, in all evangelising work we have to learn that we have not to impose our views or our personality upon other people, but rather to aid them to grow into the maturity of their personality. This we shall do, as day by day, we ourselves hold our neighbour in prayer before God, and ask what is His purpose for their lives. Thus, we with them shall enter into the vision of God and so become His servants now on earth and in His Mercy citizens of His kingdom in heaven.

CHRISTIANITY AND EDUCATION
(The substance of an address delivered
at the Conference)

The Abbot of Pershore and Nashdom

I confess I feel myself something of a Rip Van Winkle coming thus to address a group of schoolmasters on an aspect of their educational business after having been for many years out of touch with the educational world. But perhaps I may say, by way of justification, that Van Winkle's long sleep did not leave him unchanged; and so, during these years when I have had little direct contact with the educational world, my business as a confessor has brought me into very close contact with many souls and has kept before my mind many questions which have a close relationship with the business of education.

The subject upon which I am to speak to you, "Christianity and Education", is, as you know, not of my own choosing and so, perhaps, I can best approach it by examining its terms. How shall we define "Education"? Shall we say, borrowing an idea from a book which is, I suppose, now out of date—*Natural Law in the Spiritual World*—that Education is the process by which we fit the personality for its most profitable reaction with its environment? This, of course, at once raises questions of a fundamental character: What is the most profitable reaction with our environment? or Who makes the most profitable reaction? A Napoleon? An American millionaire? or a Saint Francis of Assisi? Our answer to this question must depend upon what we consider to be man's environment.

It is just at this point that we begin to consider education from a Christian point of view. To the Christian—to all Christians—man's environment is not only a physical one, it is spiritual also; not spiritual only, and not physical only, but both physical and spiritual. And man's business in this world is so to use his time in this double environment as to come to his true end, which is eternal life with God. The moment any scheme of education loses sight of this it ceases to be Christian and so falls outside our discussion.

Christian opinion through the centuries leaves no trace of doubt in our minds as to the true answer to the question we looked at just now; Saint Francis was the one who made the most profitable reaction to his environment. But if you all start training your pupils to imitate closely the manner of life of Saint Francis, I fancy the chances of retaining your posts will be small. That sort of thing would not be popular with most of the parents of your boys, and, I suppose, the schoolmaster must have some regard for what parents require or expect.

But what is Christianity? Many answers are offered to this question, but most of them are, at best, only partial. Perhaps the commonest of these regards Christianity as a code of behaviour. There is, of course, a Christian code of behaviour, but to identify Christianity with behaviour is to rob it of its most distinctive and most inspiring elements. Even if we grant that Christian conduct is possible without the other elements of the Christian religion, we shall be obliged, I think, to acknowledge that the type of character so produced would be anything but typically Christian.

Similarly, there are tendencies to limit Christianity to its expression in certain modes of worship, "High" or "Low"; and the excessive emphasis laid upon such matters has produced a great deal of very un-Christian bitterness. On the other hand, of those who are accounted the choicest exemplars of Christian character some have worshipped God in the bareness of the desert and others in the splendour of the richest cathedrals.

And, once more, Christianity is not to be identified with assent to a certain set of dogmatic statements. Some of the most learned doctors of theology have not shown themselves remarkable for sanctity. Indeed, it is a commonplace of

Christian spirituality that it is better to serve God in howsoever humble a way than to be able to talk learnedly about Him.

No! Christianity is the right relation of the innermost citadel of the personality to God; it therefore transcends particular manifestations whether in act, external worship, or intellectual definition. I believe psychologists used to call this citadel of the personality the "Transcendental Ego"; they may do so still for all I know. Shall we, for our present purpose, speak of it as the "Soul"?

It is the training of the soul that the Christian teacher must keep in view; education apart from this end is not Christian education, however expert it may be, and however successful from the point of view of examinations or worldly careers. The soul is influenced to a greater or less degree by every phenomenon in its environment, and hence arises the need for a definitely Christian atmosphere in the school—Christian masters; books written from a Christian point of view, especially on such a subject as history, though even books on the physical sciences can make their contribution; definite instruction in the Christian Religion. And, further, the soul is modified by every one of its volitional acts, and therefore a careful training in Christian habits is of first importance. Here again, the necessity of Christian teachers is obvious.

To come to your own particular problem, how are you to make the education you give to your pupils a Christian education? In the first place, I think you must remember that the responsibility is not wholly yours. Your pupils come to you partly formed and there are other contributions besides your own to their further development. There are, for example, the other masters and the other boys; and I am sure that I shall receive your whole-hearted approval when I say that, in many cases, the good done at school in term time is undone at home during the vacations.

No! the responsibility is not wholly yours. But you can only discharge such part of it as is yours by being yourselves simply as good Christians as you can be. You have a duty to discharge by teaching such and such subjects as well as you can, with the immediate aim of bringing your pupils up to a certain standard of proficiency. This is your first responsibility. But if you are yourselves doing your utmost to live a Christian life and to deal with your pupils always in Christian fashion, you will be doing all you can as individuals to give the Christian atmosphere and training of which we have seen the need. Your pupils will learn more from you than the subjects of your lessons; they will experience the attraction of the Christian life and character, an attraction, that is to say, towards their true end.

INDEX